D0908537

PAINTING FOR PLEASURE

Buildings in Winter

PAINTING

=== FOR ===

PLEASURE

By

MORRIS DAVIDSON

BOSTON

CHARLES T. BRANFORD

Publishers

PRINTED IN THE UNITED STATES OF AMERICA
BY THE COLONIAL PRESS INC., CLINTON, MASS.

To ANNE

PREFACE

The aims of this book are several. As the title suggests, it proposes to open a new recreational field to those who have found non-creative hobbies unsatisfying. To paint for pleasure means to the author to paint with definite esthetic objectives as well as with some command of the medium. These objectives are considered as fully as are the technical means and procedures.

A second aim is to provide a brief outline of composition for those amateurs who have painted for some years but without basic ideas. Even among professional painters the knowledge of composition is not infrequently vague or haphazard. The exposition of space composition and the exercises which follow will, it is hoped, be of use to many painters as well as to amateurs.

For purposes of simplification and convenient reference the book is divided into two parts: the first, a manual of procedure for beginners; the second, the outline of composition. The point of view expressed throughout is evolved from modern painting.

The ultimate aim of the book is cultural in a general sense. The author believes that a vital national art can exist only where there is a public educated to certain standards, and that a participation more active than sitting at lectures will create such a public.

The material here offered and its manner of presentation has as its authority only the experience of one who has enjoyed teaching mature persons to paint and has seen their development from awkward, struggling novices to painters of interesting pictures.

M. D.

CONTENTS

LIST OF ILLUSTRATIONS

PLATES IN COLOR

PLATES IN MONOCHROME

xi

TEXT ILLUSTRATIONS

PART I
A Manual for Beginners

I

THE RÔLE OF THE AMATEUR PAINTER

MANY MORE Americans than ever before, particularly in the larger cities, are taking up painting as a hobby. The ready inference is that this amateur activity in art is only a new fad or fancy which will soon spend itself. I should hate to think that this were so and that I am doing nothing more in putting forth this volume than adding a player's manual to an extensive literature on bridge. It is my conviction that the desire to paint for pleasure is an indication of a changing social attitude—nothing revolutionary but portentous nevertheless. It is my purpose to show the open-minded reader that there is something more than distraction or mild enjoyment to be gained from a hobby that invites a most satisfying exercise—that of the creative consciousness.

Some of us play games to kill time, for want of something better to do. Others make play the reason or basis for their social life. Still others play games for the excitement of gambling, the competitive instinct, the exultation of victory, and so on. Painting is a very different kind of activity. It certainly kills time but in doing so inherits the victim's best legacy—accomplishment. It may very well be a social activity but it ends without the usual unflattering commentaries on one's friends after their departure. In place of gambling it offers the thrill of discovery; in place of competition, a challenge to one's own powers; in place of victory, the satisfaction of saying something original that will remain, at least until you yourself destroy it.

No activity is more stimulating to original thought and formation of opinion. This is because the process of making a picture is an exercise in inductive logic. Every step grows out of the one before it. The painter is his own judge of facts, his eyes are his authority. Only his own decision determines what he does with his brush. And so he unconsciously cultivates the habit of independence and reliance upon his own mind and sense-responses.

In this respect alone painting is a much more cultural activity than passive hobbies such as, for example, book-collecting of first editions. The worth of any such collected object is established in a commercial market, and despite the proud assertions of the collector that he has an innate cultural bent for old and rare editions, it is your privilege to believe that he is only indulging (1) a form of pride in possession, (2) a gambling instinct for future values, (3) a vicarious sense of greatness in owning the works of great persons. The values given to an amateur's painting, on the other hand, are given by the amateur alone, and perhaps his friends.

There is no doubt that the enormous growth, since the great depression, of cultural activities, particularly among adult educational groups, is due to the physical limitation of ambition for wealth. Materially the average intelligent American is in an impasse, a blind alley. He is no longer satisfied with playing games, first because games no longer reflect the adventurous state of his workaday mind, second because life itself is dependent upon the hope of expansion. If you cannot expand materially, you will try to expand mentally, spiritually. Painting offers this expansion more than any other activity, for it leaves tangible evidence of accomplishment besides the experience itself.

The creative hobby, then, is supplanting the time-killing game. The competitive spirit in recreation, the exultation of victory, is being rejected in favor of a more lasting and more satisfying reward, the pleasure derived from making something beautiful, from creating something out of nothing, from organizing pictorially fragmentary and chaotic impressions. Pragmatist philosophers have blindly and systematically opposed the exercise of real esthetic faculties. They have spread the dogma that any operation well done is beautiful. But lawyers who have conducted "beautiful" cases beautifully, and surgeons who have many times performed "beautiful" operations are today turning to painting for the satisfaction of esthetic impulses. There is something mentally and spiritually restorative in the satisfying of that impulse (as some philosophers would discover if they could be persuaded to begin humbly).

But merely to put on a painter's smock and to play at being an artist will not bring the tired brainworker that sense of personal expansion and restorative action which he would like. There must be definite objectives in this creative play, definite rules. To try to recapture the aimless wandering and adventure of the child mind will lead only to a sense of futility. The finished work, finished only because the worker has reached complete boredom, will remain a reproach to the intelligent person capable of being moved by a work of art. *Esthetic satisfaction can be had only when the hobbyist feels that his efforts are related in some way to the worth-while pictures he has seen.* Whether he ultimately achieves a work of art or not, he must feel that he is aiming at a work of art if not in precisely the same way, at least with the same objectives with which great artists approach a canvas.

What are these objectives? They are the subject of this

book. But before we begin a discourse upon them, it is necessary to point out that while the objectives are the same, there is a vital difference in the psychological processes of attaining them. The artist works almost entirely subconsciously as far as esthetic principles are concerned, finding with each stroke of the brush a point of departure for the next. Rules do not exist for him. Each work of art has its own rules. His language is so fluent that he may devote himself entirely to effective expression. The hobbyist on the other hand has no knowledge of painting grammar or idiom to begin with. He has presumably no background of introspective living, no objective detachment from humanity with the consequent contemplative habit. The urge to make order out of chaos, compulsive with the artist, will be to the hobbyist more in the nature of a mental problem. For these reasons and no doubt many others, the psychological attitude will be different. *The objectives for the beginner will have to be conscious, intellectual, strictly formulated in advance.*

It follows naturally that the product of artist and that of amateur will bear the stamp of the process by which each is created. The objectives, which we will call plastic elements, remain the same; but the "feeling" conveyed to the spectator will be very different indeed. It will be too readily observed that the difference in the emotional power of the two works is the difference in technical skill, craftsmanship, etc., which the artist has perfected over many years. But actually this is not the case. Emotional power or feeling is like the tone of a violin. It is in the instrument. The instrument must be fine, it must be aged by the action of atmosphere, called time. In the case of the fine artist it is, to be exact, not time but felt experience which imparts a necessary quality to the fine instrument.

These differences are sketchily mentioned because an

undertaking such as painting for pleasure too often ends in disillusion, or what is worse, a kind of crackpot superiority in which the hobbyist feels he is in reality a great artist misunderstood. The amateur should be happy in the thought that his simple exercises with paint are not only giving him pleasure but are fitting him for an appreciation of painting more valid and durable than that derived from books and lectures. The amateur painter may stand before a work of art as inarticulate as ever but he will follow its processes, detect the logic in its unique laws, speculate on the reasons for the artist's choice of a passage of color, a shape; in short, live the work over again as if he himself had done it. He will realize, however, that a work of art is distinguished from an intelligent painting not by superior knowledge or technique but by the felt force of the painter's personality, his new and original point of view.

The difference between artist and hobbyist is dwelt upon at perhaps too great length because of the distinct difference in the social rôle of each. There are many who are concerned only and ultimately with the pleasure they may derive from practicing the art and who like to feel that they are above and beyond social rôles. But they play them nevertheless, if not deliberately then unconsciously. It should be a source of gratification to any amateur to know that it is himself and others like him who affect the country's art quite as much as do the professionals, if less directly. This is because there can be no great productivity of fine painting without a greater productivity of mediocre painting. The great artists of history are those few who have made use of the lessons and experience of the many. The keen support necessary to sustain the adventurous and revolutionary professional in his search and research can be provided only by the sympathetic amateur. Thus the greater the number of intelligent amateurs of painting the greater the possibility that fine artists will receive just recognition, the greater the incentive to professionals to soar above their supporters. And the finer the national art.

If the hobbyist impatiently rejects this social rôle, let him at least look with respect (if not deference) upon the work of the serious professional. In private life he may think himself Dr. Johnson; but in the presence of the real Dr. Johnson he must be only Mr. Boswell. If he pits himself against the artist, he runs the danger of becoming rutted, reactionary, smug—a hindrance to the good artist instead of his most helpful ally.

So much for the part the amateur is to play. Throughout this book differentiation will be made between the good picture—good because competent and intelligent—and the work of art. The beginner should restrict his painting to the simple objectives in the exercises outlined rather than try to imitate the examples of art put before him for analysis. Eventually he will reach the point at which art begins. Imitation then will cease to be alluring; the personality will want to express its unique self.

A word as to the manner of using this manual. The painter-for-pleasure should work at least twice a week. He will find it difficult to sustain his interest, keep his study "warm," if he works less frequently. One evening and one afternoon make an excellent arrangement as the afternoon period will permit him to experience the handling of color in daylight, quite a different thing from color under "daylight" electric lamps. If possible he should get together a small group of congenial friends for one of the sessions, and work alone in the other. The group will be a great stimulation, although there is always the risk of its sociability becoming the primary interest. A good plan for group work is to declare regular five-minute rest periods in each half hour and to restrict conversation (and smoking and drinking) to these periods. The stimulation of seeing how others treat or solve the problems one is struggling with is practically essential for survival through the early stages. Even when the student has learned to control his color and brush, he will need the objective criticism of his fellow worker. The basis of criticism it is the intention of this book to provide, but the application of it will depend upon the clear mind and the accurate eye. For this reason it will be well to make frequent trips to galleries to see how professional painters *see*. It will also prove profitable to have an artist criticize the group work. Such criticism should not be too frequent nor should the same artist be invited to criticize more than twice consecutively. The difference between a painter who teaches and a teacher of painting is that the former is often "sot in his ways" and is morally convinced that the best that can happen to the student is to fall into the habit of imitating the master without question. The teacher of painting on the other hand is interested in the free development of the individual with no restrictions except those imposed by esthetic principles. If the student cannot find the latter type, he should beware the tight grip of the former.

With these few warnings delivered—all offered in the interest of painting for pleasure—we may now turn to the proper business of this book, how to proceed. First let us give a brief moment to the practical matter of supplies.

II

WORKING CONDITIONS AND MATERIALS

THE ROOM in which the group is to work may have windows on any side except that which faces the afternoon sun. Sunlight is yellowish and distorts color in the same way that a pair of sunglasses will. Proper lighting for night work is still a matter of debate; blue bulbs of course are necessary to approximate the cool rays of north light but the manner of their arrangement is so far experimental. The writer has found it practicable, in his own night classes, to use the following method: The ceiling is painted white. Somewhere near the center a droplight is fitted with a 300 or 500 watt daylight lamp. A sheet metal cone about two feet in diameter and enameled white on the inside is suspended in such a way that the bulb is invisible from any point in the room. The light is reflected from the ceiling. Additional outlets may be installed or the light supplemented by smaller cones perched above doorways or mouldings and tilted upward toward the center. The soft quality of the indirect lighting will be enhanced by painting the walls of the room a cool light gray.

Equipment need not be elaborate. Of greater importance is sufficient space in which to move about. A vacant room is much more satisfactory than a romantically cluttered-up studio. No rugs or carpets should be left on the floor as the drippings and scrapings of oil and pigment will be hard to control. An old pail or metal container should be provided for discarded paint rags and oils.

Along one side of the room a long table or improvised shelf will be almost indispensable. Upon it will be set paint boxes, oil and turpentine containers, paint rags, etc. Each worker should provide himself with a paint box, a high stool upon which to rest either his palette or himself, and an easel. The easel should be of the single vertical, T base type. Its average price is five dollars. All tripods are unsatisfactory. Facility in raising and lowering the canvas as well as in tilting it makes the vertical easel superior.

The paint box should be 12″ x 16″ inside and be fitted with canvas boards of that size. There will be grooves for three. These boards are usually 20¢ each. The box itself, equipped with palette, can be bought for an average price of $3. Under no circumstances permit the salesman to sell you a completely fitted or equipped box. The elaborate contents will be very nearly useless. Instead, order the following: 1 palette knife, 35¢; 1 small bottle turpentine, 15¢; 1 small bottle raw linseed oil, 15¢; 1 oil cup, 10¢; 6 flat bristle brushes of good make, 1 No. 2, 2 No. 4, 2 No. 6 and 1 No. 8, average price for total $3.

Pigment is the principal difficulty for the unguided or misguided beginner. Not only are many colors chemically incompatible, but their composition and grinding are so far from standard that one must rely on famous brands to feel assured of quality. Yet such brands are often prohibitively priced. The beginner must keep in mind that he will, for a considerable time, waste paint rather than use it, and will save himself more than half the cost of his equipment by refraining from imported brands. Nevertheless he must avoid the cheapest makes, the "decorators' " colors which are loaded with clay and the fatty jelly produced by adding a large percentage of aluminum stearate to the pure pigment. Even pure colors are often so poorly ground as to be almost useless. The pigment coagulates and floats in oil when it is hastily and unevenly ground.

Colors are permanent, impermanent, or permanent when restricted to certain combinations with other colors. There is no such thing as a semi-permanent color which a large British house so honestly advertises. The safest colors to use are not the very best or most expensive but those which are chemically most compatible. For this reason the student is advised to limit his palette to the list given below.

"What brand of paint should I use?" Every good dealer will carry a make of paint of fair quality and reasonable price and one can do no better than rely on the colorman's judgment. Sometimes these brands are made locally and are equal to the best imported makes. More often they are second grade products made by reputable manufacturers and distributed under a different name. These pigments are the same as the first grade pigments, but they have been greatly diluted by the addition of stearate fillers. And while they are sold with the guarantee of being permanent and with the assertion that the filler is absolutely inert, the truth is that these clay and metal precipitates are sure to affect the linseed oil in which the pigment is ground. I do not for this reason advise against the use of such paint. I believe it is good enough for students provided they are careful to restrict the use of linseed oil to the very minimum.

There is no such thing as perfect paint. An artist will find certain colors of one make more suitable to his technique than any other and yet look to other brands for other colors. After twenty years of experimentation I have come down to four makes of paint, each superior to the others in certain colors.

Every painter will have evolved his own notion of a perfect

WORKING CONDITIONS AND MATERIALS 13

palette or list of colors for beginners. A painter can walk through an art school and tell very nearly which colors the instructors insist upon by looking at the array of paintings or studies in each room. The palette is often a source of permanent bitterness between instructors. The student's use of a forbidden color will appear to his teacher a serious disloyalty and invite that cutting sarcasm for which art teachers are noted. The fact is a painter can make use only of his own set of colors just as one can speak only in one's own voice. (To rationalize arguments in defense of one's voice appears to us egoistic.) The best any instructor can do is to say, "This is my palette. In the course of time you will want to add to it and change it. Each person will find he has an affinity for certain colors and combinations of color."

With this reservation for the future I set down in two columns lists of desirable colors for beginners. In the left column appears a professional painter's equipment, in the right the nearest equivalent list (called figuratively "palette") of less expensive pigments, quite adequate for those whose budgets for hobbies are limited:

Ultramarine Red	Alizarin Crimson
Cadmium Red	Vermilion
Cadmium Orange	Chrome Orange
Cadmium Yellow Med.	Chrome Yellow Med.
Zinc Yellow	Zinc Yellow
Zinc White	Zinc White
Cobalt Blue	Cobalt Blue
Ultramarine Blue	Ultramarine Blue
Emeraude or Viridian	Emeraude or Viridian

These are the prismatic colors, the nearest hues to the pure light of the prism. Accept no substitutes. Buy the studio size tubes. The price for the complete list will range from four dollars for satisfactory pigment to fourteen dollars for really fine pigment.

A few additional items will be found necessary, not in painting, but in preparing the beginner for his first combat with paint. A drawing board, a pad of charcoal paper, a half dozen thumb tacks, six sticks each of hard and very soft charcoal, an emery block, a chamois skin and kneaded eraser, a bottle of fixatif and a simple atomizer (total about $2.50) are indispensable. Old shirts or sheets for paint rag, conveniently cut and folded, round out the list of supplies.

The use of the articles listed will be made clear in the descriptions of procedures. Certain matters pertaining to the care and preservation of equipment, however, had better be considered here. The palette must be kept clean and smooth. If much paint remains on it after the working session, this pigment can be transferred to a strip of glass which is kept submerged in water. The water will prevent rapid oxidization and hardening of the paint. The palette should be wiped with a clean paint rag moistened with oil.

Brushes are good for a decade if properly kept. Upon finishing work they should be rinsed in clean turpentine and oil and then washed. If it is inconvenient to wash them at once, they may be wrapped tightly in paint rags. Within a few hours they should be washed carefully in lukewarm water and soap. The paint is apt to lodge at the base of the bristles, and most brushes are made unfit for use by the careless habit of washing only the tips. To dislodge the paint each brush should be worked in a lather in the palm of the hand and between thumb and forefinger. The brushes should be rinsed before putting away, although some painters believe a slightly soapy brush to be more pliable than a clean one.

The use of the palette knife will be indicated from time to time. It is an indispensable instrument. It serves not only to lift and transfer paint, but it makes possible the use of the palette itself. The small area of the palette would be altogether inadequate if it were not for the knife. The painter is constantly removing one batch of color to make room for the mixing of another batch. In addition to this use, the palette knife is the tool for scraping from the canvas the painter's mistakes and unwanted accidental effects. Care should be taken not to cut or puncture the canvas with the rounded point of the knife. Experience will teach the proper angle for scraping and the proper pressure for mixing pigment.

A useful tool to carry in the paintbox is a small pair of flat pliers. At times the caps of the tubes of paint become "frozen" and the painter is greatly annoyed by the delay and futile effort in attempting to loosen them. The pliers do the work in a jiffy.

Before leaving this dry matter of working conditions and materials it might be well to say a word on the stance and position of draughtsman and painter. Drawing may be done from a sitting position, but painting never. This is because color values are far more difficult to relate than black and white values. The relationship of color values is such a delicate and deceptive affair that the painter must allow himself ample room for standing as far back from his canvas as his canvas is from the study. Half closing the eyes will, of course, obviate to some extent the need for all this space. But the beginner often has difficulty in looking through a squint, whereas distance from his canvas will lend not enchantment but greater accuracy of vision.

The draughtsman, then, may sit at his drawing board while the painter stands. The top edge of the board rests against the table, the bottom rests on or in his lap. But there is no rule for his sitting. If he prefers to stand, he may fix the board on his easel, tilt it back slightly, and work so.

The painter stands at arm's length from his canvas. It is a good plan for the beginner to place the high stool between himself and his work to prevent him from committing the common fault of putting his nose to his canvas. For some unexplained reason many beginners will creep up on their paintings and soon become hopeless nigglers.

Niggling is an excellent term for the painter's vocabulary. It means a picayune technique, an absorption in trifling details, a tendency to overcautious working, a killing of all freshness of stroke and color by laborious repainting and overpainting. And it is found to go along with the myopic stance.

A problem in arrangement of easels arises when a group is working from the same model or still-life subject. The amateur will be apt to place his easel in front of the study, his canvas parallel to it. But such an arrangement will be unfair to his fellows, since it will exclude them from a good view. The practical arrangement will be to make all the easels radiate from the study like the spokes of a wheel so that each canvas shall form a right angle to the study. Each painter will look at the study by slightly turning his head. His body will face his canvas. Collisions can be avoided by putting these radiating easels at different distances from the study so that there will be room for the painter to step back.

Things *not* to use can be briefly enumerated. A mahl-stick is the prop of Hollywood artists, as are velvet jackets. A diminishing glass is a self-deceiving instrument which prettifies the poorest daubs. Sable brushes are mostly for retouchers and craftsmen.

And now we are ready to begin.

III

SIMPLE DRAWING AS PREPARATION

It is commonly believed that all great artists, when only four years old, drew perfect portraits of their grandmothers. The natural ability to draw or copy what is before one is universally accepted as evidence of artistic ability. And so it may be, to a very limited extent. More accurately it is only an indication of plastic sensibility—an aptitude for coördinating hand and eye and memory in reproduction of the seen object. In itself skill in drawing does not necessarily make an artist, although lack of such skill in an artist would indicate that he entered upon his vocation at a late date and may never quite catch up. Most artists are excellent draughtsmen because the aptitude for drawing was manifested at an early age, encouraged and developed. But there are many instances of artists acquiring a command of drawing in their maturity.

The lack of this aptitude in the grown-up who wishes to paint should therefore discourage him not at all. The principal difficulty for him will be the coördination of hand and eye. He will see things one way and put them down another. Practice will reëducate nervous and mental and muscular responses. But because such discipline is slow and painful, the adult will find it necessary to rely upon intellectual processes a good deal more than does, for example, the schoolboy. All literal delineation of contour is a matter of resolving objects into simple geometric forms. The grown-up who fears he will never be able to draw a straight line will find, by practicing

17

the exercises at the end of this chapter, that he will soon be able to draw any simple thing that is put before him.

What is far more important than the ability to copy the correct contour of objects is the ability to see pictures. By this is meant the ability to see the grouping and interrelation of things rather than to see things individually. The habit of seeing pictures must be formed by the student at once, whether he can draw or not, for on it depends his progress as a painter.

The making of pictures is not in itself accomplished by rules or even by a knowledge of the procedures and devices used by great painters. These are ultimately indispensable but the first requisite is the faculty of seeing pictures in nature. Some persons may see more than others in a given time. A popular newspaper puzzle or game exists by which a reader may test his ability to note a number of facts set down in a picture. This is one kind of seeing, and it is indeed a commendable accomplishment. The kind of seeing required for picture-making, however, is very different. The number of facts has no bearing on this seeing; the selection of *the fact* which graphically describes and which is of interest only when combined with other similar, descriptive facts is the requirement for visual picture-making. To grasp this difference more clearly, let us consider a tree. When we look at the tree in the ordinary way we may see that it is forty feet high and of the nut family. We note the texture of the bark, the shape of its leaves, the hole in the trunk, a parade of red ants on one of its limbs, a broken branch and a badly pruned stump. But if we look at the tree pictorially we take in another set of facts: the conformation of the masses of foliage, their color in light and shade, the curved lines of the branches, their relation to each other. Once a person has developed the habit of such pictorial seeing he will be on the way to making

pictures. The rules and practices of composition will then
become vital necessities for effective statement.

Before we make pictures on our drawing paper or canvas,
we must make them with actual objects. It is not only necessary to attain a nice recording of the objects; it is essential
that the objects be first arranged in such a way as to provide
pictorial possibilities. We look about for a few objects which
we say appeal to our eye. The problem is to arrange them in
such a way that they evoke interest, based on variety and difference—the opposite of monotony. Fortunately, the objects
we have selected are different from each other in size, shape,
and color. There is a red book, a yellow sugar bowl, and a
little Mexican glass pitcher of indigo blue. If we had just
three oranges to arrange, the problem of making an interesting group would tax the artist's compositional skill. But with
such dissimilar and attractive objects monotonous arrangement would hardly be possible. At least, it appears so. But
what if we were to string these differently colored, differently
shaped objects out in a line as in Figure 1. The stick of charcoal is no respecter of color and reduces all color to *value*
(degree of light or dark). The values, it is true, are different
—light bowl, darker book, and darkest pitcher. Yet there is
something disturbingly monotonous about this arrangement,
and we shall have to find out what it is.

First of all, each object stands by itself. Equal intervals of
space separate the end objects from the center one. There is
therefore no suggestion of relationship. We do not see these
objects as a picture; instead we *read* them, from left to right.
The process of reading is very different from the process of
seeing pictures. When we read, the mind is a kind of adding
machine which sums up all the words and the individual
meanings of words and sends us the result or conclusion. (Of
course when we read poetry or fine prose, more than mere

statement is involved; we feel and taste the words individually and in combination. But ordinary reading is only for information.) In seeing pictures we cannot proceed from one part or unit to another in any formulated order. We must see the conclusion first and the means for arriving at it afterward. Instead of enumerating the objects in a picture or taking an inventory of them, we see a single statement in which each object has meaning only in relation to everything else in the picture. If this were not so there would be no sense in making pictures of definite sizes. If you take a big canvas and paint an excellent likeness of a horse and a dog on one side of it, leaving the other half blank, and then put a frame around it, will you have a picture? Decidedly not. A picture is determined by the use made of the *area* on which the objects are depicted. Or to put it another way, the singleness of feeling conveyed by a picture is conditioned by the use made of the complete area. If the objects are placed in this area in an inventive manner, and if the area is thereby divided into varied shapes or pattern, there is a likelihood that the result will be a picture.

Of course there is a great deal more to pictorial composition than simple arrangement of an area, or pattern. A fine composition may be in itself art. If we cannot begin by making art, we can at least begin by making pictures. For this, pattern will for the time being suffice.

In order to cut up the area of our canvas into interesting shapes we add to our objects a strip of green material and a white cloth, a dish towel. With these as background and foreground we shall have little difficulty in picking out patterns or shapes with which to cut up the blank areas. Since we want as much variety as possible, we place the objects on different levels suggesting space between them. We lay the book down at an angle because the diagonal lines so formed

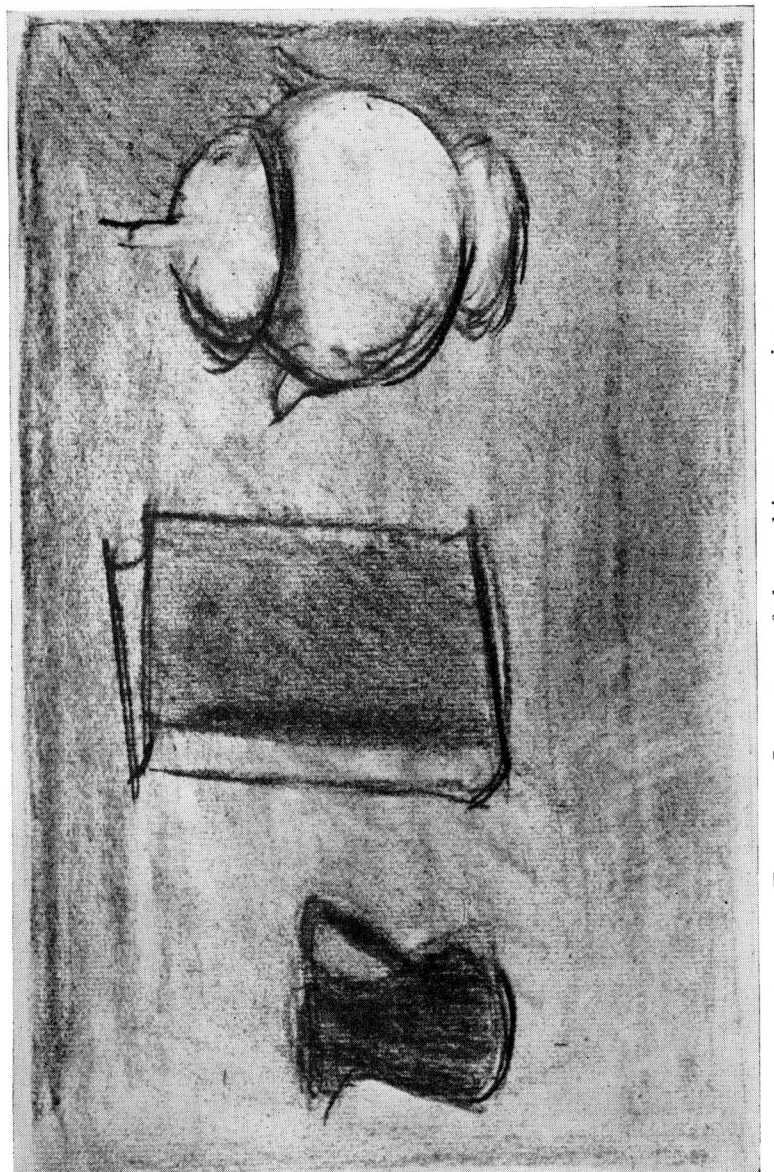

FIGURE 1.—Inventory of three objects, not a picture

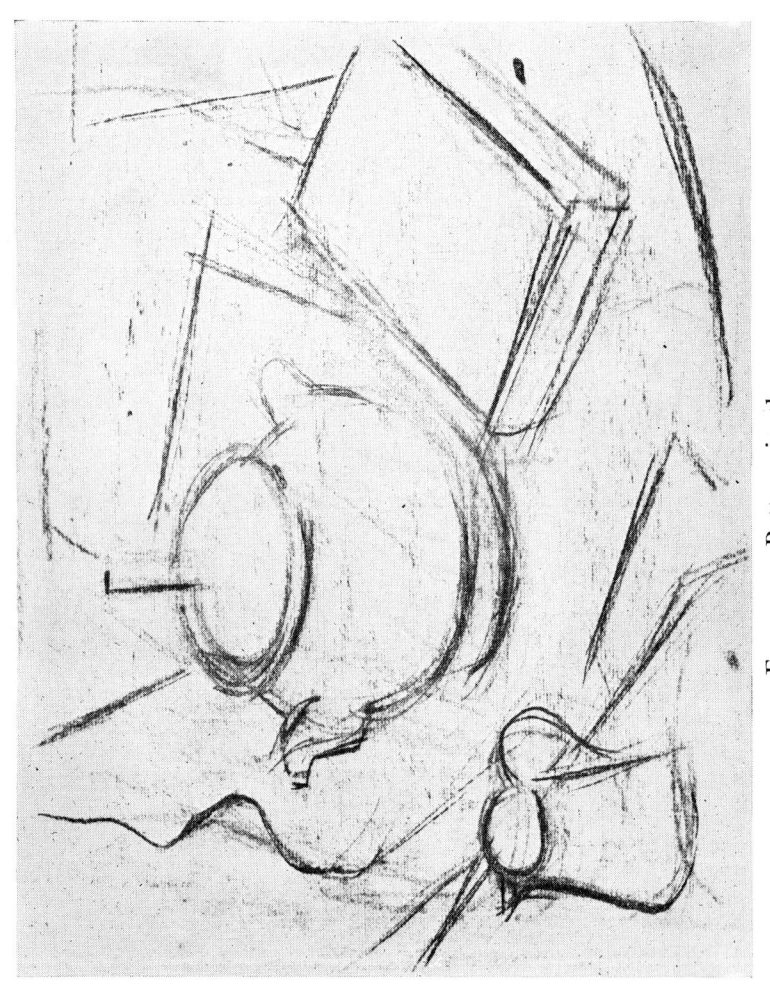

FIGURE 2.—Pattern in the area

are not only more interesting than vertical or horizontal lines but also because they suggest recession. They give a feeling of depth. The folds of material make other lines and divisions. And the whole study is placed below the level of the eye to prevent the objects from appearing strung out.

However difficult it may be for some individuals to delineate objects, the task of reproducing objects tonally will not be beyond their capabilities. By this tonal or "smudge" method the outline of an object is built up from the inside: that is to say, it is only the delimitation of the mass of the object. If this appears abstruse it will soon become clear as we proceed with the drawing of the still life. Our first task is to limit the area of the picture.

A sheet of charcoal paper is firmly tacked to the drawing board. A margin of an inch or more is drawn on all sides. The area thus made is filled in completely by a light even tone of gray made by rubbing the soft charcoal over the surface and working it into the grain of the paper with the palm and fingers. The flat even tone should not be much darker than pearl, nor should it be worked into the paper too energetically. (See that the hands are free from oiliness.)

The area determined, the next step is to place the objects in such a way that they fill it while yet maintaining correct relationships (proportions) to each other. The usual fault of beginners is their tendency to make the objects tiny so that they appear lost in the area. In placing the objects the freest and sketchiest scribbling is permissible as the soft charcoal can be removed with the wipe of a finger or with the chamois. Figure 2 shows this first stage, the placing of the objects in the area. Note that the background is roughly divided into shapes or patterns.

Our next objective is a double one. We must divide the entire area into patterns of dark and light and we must state accurately the light and dark relation of the objects to each other. This might appear a complicated business. But, half closing our eyes so that we see only through a squint which eliminates detail, we find that there are various definite degrees of light and dark. These are the values. We note which object as an entirety is the lightest and which the darkest value, ignoring highlights, reflections and accents. (The painter speaks of an object being a "value" in the same way that he speaks of it being a color.) Each object is seen as a flat pattern, the background and foreground as other flat patterns. The bowl appears to be the lightest, the little pitcher the darkest object. The book is halfway. These values cannot be established without taking into account the values of the material surrounding the objects. The white cloth is, together with the light edge of the book, even lighter than the bowl, and this cloth will be the number one value. From here on the process is one of adjustment of relations. Where more dark is required, more charcoal is added and rubbed in until it stays put. Where the tone is too dark, it may be lifted with a light pass of the chamois. This is the second stage of the drawing—pattern and relative values.

The objective of the final stage is *form* or *volume*, the sense of the third dimension. This feeling of the third dimension in painting is called tactile value by the noted critic Berenson. Speaking of his responses to pictures, he says, "I must have the illusion of varying muscular sensations inside my palm and fingers corresponding to the various projections of this figure, before I shall take it for granted as real . . ." The essential in the art of painting, he believes, is "to stimulate our consciousness of tactile values, so that the picture shall have at least as much power as the object represented."

Note that he says, "*at least* as much power as the object represented." A good painting must have a great deal more power than the object represented. A painting of an object is an abstraction, an editorial opinion, an intensification of that object, and if it is the tactile value the painter wishes to convey, he must convey it unequivocally, purified, magnified. This he does by an intellectual process of simplification of tactile values. He reduces the object to planes.

The almost imperceptible gradations of shading which make an object appear round to the eye can be very nearly reproduced by the painter or draughtsman. But the camera will do it more exactly. Yet the photographed object, however interestingly done, will fail to have volume or tactile value. Instead of recreating the object for us it will only be reminiscent of the object; or else it will give us an extravagant statement of its surface texture. The reasons for the inadequacy of the exact reproduction of the object are psychological. In a room we see all objects in relation to all others. But if we focus our attention upon any single object or group of objects, it will gradually exclude from our consciousness the objects about it. The longer we concentrate our sensibilities upon it the more we will feel it tactilely. Isolating the "feel" of the object intensifies its form, its color, its reality. (This is not at all the same thing as looking at the object inventorially.) The camera, not being subjective, can only record the object as a fragment of a panorama of objects even when it is arranged in a composition and specially lighted. But the painter who has looked at the object long enough to feel it will be doing a very trifling thing by recording the lights and shadows with literal reference to its fragmentary and accidental aspects. If he has really felt the object, he will seek a way to record its permanent aspects or rather those facts about the object which give it significance and distinction from other objects. He resorts to planes.

The plane, then, is a device, an abstraction. It is a system of gradation like notes in music. It is possible to make sounds so subtly graded as to defy musical notation. The sounds in nature do this. The phonograph record and the camera record these gradations but musician and painter resolve them into a meaningful system. The plane is equivalent to the musical phrase. It is of light or dark value (or of color value) which in proper relation to other planes will convey to the eye a simplified, intensified sensation of its tactile value. If planes of light are consistently and logically placed on all objects in the study, the study will have a sense of reality very different from photographic realism.

We return now to the still-life study. Having attained a proper relationship of values, we now proceed to express the volume. We determine the source of light, which is of course the same for all three objects, and make a light plane or band of light in the correct place. This plane of light must be subtly done so that it will lie convincingly in the flat value given each object. Then we add the planes of dark. We minimize the importance of reflected lights, and even highlights, because these are accidental while the large planes give the permanent quality, the form, of each object. The charcoal drawing, Figure 3, illustrates this third stage of a smudge drawing made as a preparatory study for a painting.

If the beginner works in this fashion he will find much enjoyment in the pictorial results, the magical way in which objects spring out of darks and lights even without exact contour. Such quick results will enable the novice to summon more patience for the business of geometrical construction (explained at the end of this chapter) which he may find so boring when practiced by itself. Adequate drawing will result from the two exercises.

The phrase "exact contour" applies of course only to literal drawing. Drawing as an art begins where literal drawing stops. It is even rarer than painting as an art. But this is the subject of another chapter. Here we are concerned only with drawing as a preparation for painting. If executed with care and intelligence it will pave the way for (1) good arrangement in the painting, (2) interesting relationship of color values, (3) the attainment of form through color.

A charcoal drawing as preliminary study should therefore be a matter of course for the beginner. Not until he is satisfied with the black and white tonal statement will he be ready for the business of painting. The habit of seeing things in related planes, the painter's way of seeing, will be formed by continued practice with charcoal. Without such preliminary study and habit of seeing, the amateur painter will likely get off on the wrong foot; he will think of objects in terms of outlines filled in with color, instead of in terms of related passages of color and volumes. The faculty of quickly surveying and tabulating values, developed best by practice in smudge, should be as much a part of the painter's equipment as sight reading of music is to the professional singer.

There are a few technical matters pertaining to the handling of charcoal which may be mentioned here. Good craftsmanship is essential in this medium. The stick of charcoal should be held in the palm of the hand and the fingers closed around it. The little finger should rest lightly against the surface of the paper as the hand moves over it. Lines are made with a full sweep of the arm instead of with the fingers as when writing. The student should practice covering whole sheets of paper with quick, light diagonal lines made by moving the entire arm and flexing the wrist. The hard charcoal used for delineation must be kept constantly sharp so that edges between planes of light and dark may be clearly and exactly defined. Flat tones are sometimes covered by sharp diagonal lines similar to pen lines in order to give variety to the treatment. Use of the kneaded eraser should be restricted to small lights and light accents.

The finished drawing should be sprayed with fixatif to prevent the brushing off of the charcoal in handling. Before spraying be sure that the margins or white spaces are cleaned of accidental smudges or marks. To spray the drawing lay it flat as otherwise excess liquid will streak it. The surface on which the drawing rests should be protected from the damaging effects of the alcohol by newspapers. Take a position about two feet away from the drawing. In using the atomizer be sure to hold the two parts to form a right angle. Avoid tilting the bottle and spilling the contents. Two or three coverings of spray will dampen the paper, dampness being generally an indication of sufficient fixing. Allow the drawing to dry thoroughly before touching.

If the student is greatly annoyed by his inability to achieve passable shapes of objects and ends up with a distorted collection of lopsided objects even in smudge drawing, he had better give some time to acquiring a geometrical sense. First of all he should cover a sheet of paper with drawings (in pencil) of right angles, the legs or sides of equal length. He must practice making the angle in any position but always a right angle and always of equal sides. Upon a second sheet of paper he should assemble four of these right angles into a square. He should practice making squares. If every angle is a right angle and all the lines of equal length, the object will be a square and nothing could be more simple. The squares made, they are bisected by diagonals or verticals. He should make many more squares, converting them into octagons by lopping off their corners by lines equal in length to the horizontal and vertical sides remaining. Within this framework he may construct circles with little difficulty

(Figure 4a). All drawing is geometrical; with the artist it is unconscious, with the adult beginner it must be conscious. The eye of the beginner must become accustomed to measuring equal lengths, equal angles, equal shapes.

Having practiced making squares, octagons and circles within squares, the student may begin applying his experience to actual objects. An ellipse in the top of a vase should first be reduced to a rectangle approximating the

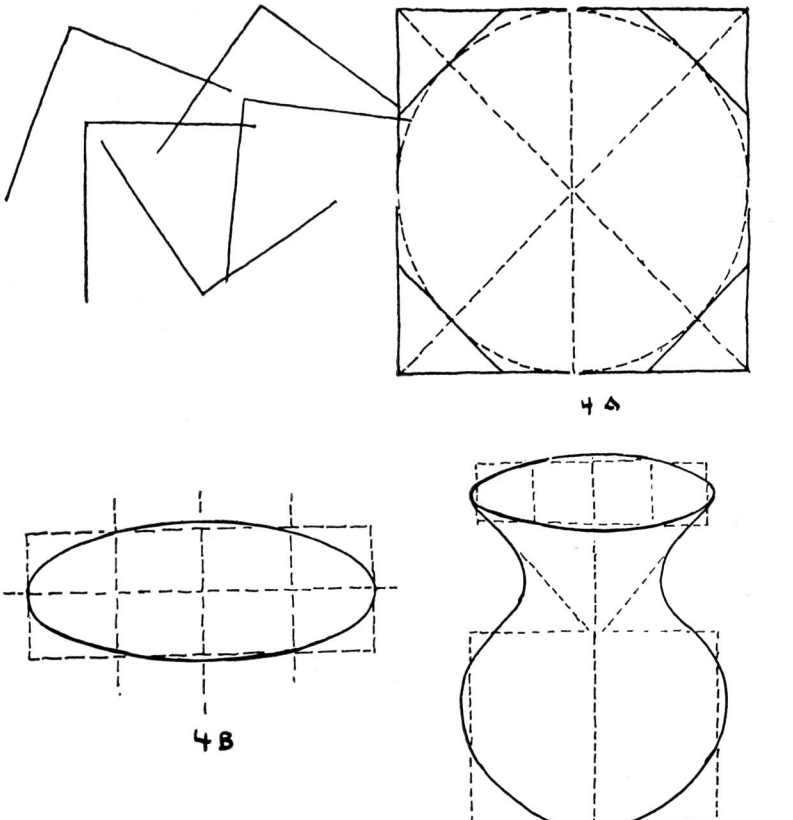

FIGURE 4.—The geometrical approach for the adult

general proportions. This rectangle is divided equally by a horizontal and a vertical and the parts subdivided by two additional verticals as in Figure 4*b*. The construction of symmetrical arcs about this framework will be a comparatively simple business. Thus the oval is correctly drawn. The whole principle of literal (as distinct from artistic) drawing lies in this procedure. In Figure 4*c* can be seen the contour of a vase framed by the simplest geometrical forms. Try this on your sketch pad.

FIGURE 3.—The preparation for the painting

IV

THE FIRST PAINTING

BEFORE attempting to translate the charcoal study into a painting it would be the better part of valor to experiment a little with pigments. For this purpose we may rule a small canvas board into rectangles 1″ x 2″. (A sheet of heavy water color paper will do if a board is not at hand.) Put a few drops of oil and an equal part of turpentine into the oil cup and attach it to the palette. Now set the palette according to the diagram below (Figure 5). (To avoid confusion, the names of pigments are those of the cheaper colors.)

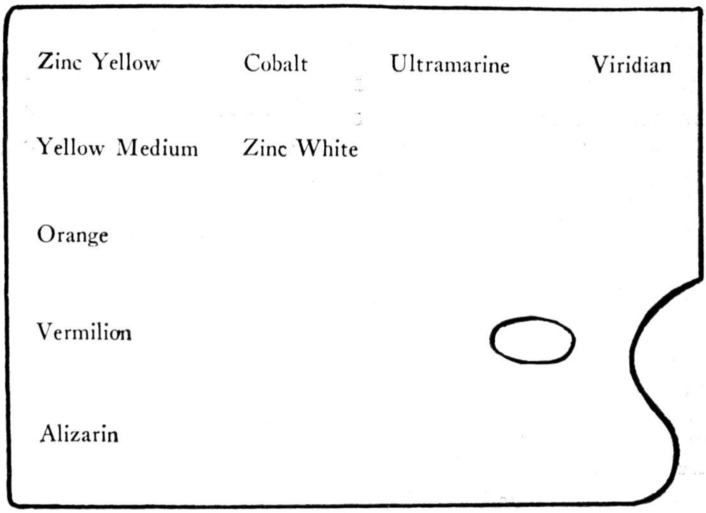

| Zinc Yellow | Cobalt | Ultramarine | Viridian |

Yellow Medium   Zinc White

Orange

Vermilion

Alizarin

FIGURE 5.—Arrangement of palette

29

A glance at the palette reveals that the colors to the left of the zinc white are lighter and brighter than those to the right. A more exact difference is expressed by the painter in the terms "warm" and "cool." The colors of fire or the sun's rays are warm; those of moonlight, the sea, shadows in sunlight, cool. It will be noted that the precise difference between the two reds, the alizarin and the vermilion, is that the first is cool, the second warm. Neither is an absolute red. One has a faint hue of blue (cool), the other a faint hue of yellow (warm). The orange is the warmest color of all. The yellow medium is also warm. But the zinc yellow (not an absolute yellow) is cold since there is in it a faint admixture of blue. It is a transitional color from yellow to yellow green. In theory red and yellow and blue are all we need. But in practice, we shall discover there are no absolutes. Pure color is only in the prism; the body of pigments is loaded with impurities. Every pigment will have a special quality and a special affinity for some other pigment. Eventually our needs will not be served by even these purest of pigments and we shall have to add at least three or four new colors. But now our objective is to acquire some notion of mixing so-called "pure" pigments; so for the time being avoiding the orange, cobalt and viridian, we shall restrict our first exercise to five colors and white.

In order to keep our colors clean we use five brushes, a brush for each color. They are dipped into the oil cup and then wiped lightly with the paint rag. Beginning in the lower left-hand corner we fill each block horizontally with the pure colors, as in Plate I. Now we go to the row above. The first half block on the left is made of the color beneath it with blue added. The half block above the blue is made of the same blue with yellow added. The intervening blocks are made of the two colors beneath each. The purple, the

PLATE I.—A simple exercise in color

orange, the green are known as secondary colors, since they are the result of mixtures of the primaries. Now we add white to our color and return to the left column. There are three blocks of red violet, all the same in color, but each lighter than the other, or higher in value. The red violet is converted to violet and successive values of blue violet. The pure yellow in the center column is raised in value twice and lowered in value with the use of blue. The blue green column is raised in value only by the addition of white. In the extreme right column are three neutral or tertiary colors. The light gray is derived from the violet and yellow green in the same horizontal line. The yellow brown below it is made from green and orange, the red brown from the cold red and blue and the warm yellow in the first line.

This chart is no spectrum. It has no design and is not even scientific. But experience has shown that complicated color charts bore adults who are eager to discover for themselves the uses and possibilities of color. It is the notion of color value that is all-important. A little experience in simple color combinations with the use of white in small and large proportion will do the student more good than so-called scientific theories.

Warning: While the chart so made will serve to introduce the beginner to the whims of pigments, its efficacy lies in *experiencing the making* of it. Merely to study the accompanying reproduction will do no good. Nor will it prove much more beneficial to hurry through the directions. The student should become sufficiently familiar with his palette to paint a second chart from memory.

Having practiced our scales we come back to the still-life study. We have the strip of green cloth suitable for background, the white cloth, the little Mexican glass of indigo blue, the book with red-orange covers, and the pale yellow sugar bowl. The matter of arrangement we attended to when we made our drawing.

We are ready to transfer the study to the canvas. We clean the palette and reset it, omitting the white. We pour out the mixture in the oil cup, clean the cup or replace it with one containing a small amount of turpentine. The brushes used for the color chart are washed thoroughly in turpentine and wiped dry. With the smallest brush the objects will be roughly placed. The brush is dipped into the turpentine and dabbed lightly into the blue. The thin watery liquid resulting will be used to outline the objects. If the outlines are wrong they can be wiped off with the paint rag. We must avoid the beginner's tendency to make the objects too small. We also remember that the space around them is to be cut into shapes as definite as the objects themselves.

The book, bowl, and glass, placed in outline, are ready for the color statement. However, it is impossible to paint one object completely without considering the colors of the things around it. All color is relative. A red surrounded by green will appear much more vivid than a red surrounded by brown. Complementary colors, or colors exactly opposed to each other, will intensify each other. The key (tonal lightness or darkness) in which the picture is to be pitched will also determine the intensity and value of the color. For example, a stained glass window in a dark picture will be much richer in intensity than the same window in a very light impressionist picture. For this reason the aim must be to cover the canvas as quickly as possible with a *tentative wash* made of paint diluted with turpentine. Such a wash is very readily removed and corrected if necessary. The color can be lightened by dabbing with the paint rag or darkened by using more pigment and less turpentine. In addition to its aid in determining the key for the painting, this wash of color dries rapidly and makes an excellent surface on which to apply thick pigment. But most important of all it is a practical way for fixing in our minds the correct color values—that is, the relation of lights and darks—so that later, when the pigment is applied more heavily, we may avoid the fumbling and changing which result in a muddy canvas.

This process of first washing in the tentative picture with turpentine is called the stain. In the stain the brushes are used with a scrubbing motion in order to work the pigment into the texture of the board or canvas, and care must be used in keeping an excessive amount of turpentine out of them. Two or three brushes will suffice, provided the painter proceeds from the lightest object or color pattern to the darkest. When the brush has once picked up a dark color it is difficult to clean it for use with lighter colors unless it is thoroughly washed in turpentine.

If the stain is done with care so that the correct relationship of the values is preserved (the test, you remember, is to look at the study with half-closed eyes eliminating all but the values), much of the struggling will be mitigated before the actual painting is begun. With no stain for preparation a few dashing, clever brush strokes may succeed in giving the illusion of the single objects, but if the values are not properly related, the picture had best be left in its imperfect, suggestive state and called a "sketch." The more the student works upon it the more muddled it will become unless he succeeds in bringing it back to the simple statement which the stain would have been in the first place. On the other hand, if the stain is done with care, all that remains for the painter to do is mix his pigment to match the stain and apply it.

In this second stage no turpentine will be used as a solvent.

This means that the light which shows through the thin pigment from the canvas itself will be obscured and will have to be *mixed into the color* by adding white. The thick pigment will be loosened by a drop of linseed oil, or better yet, the zinc white will be whipped up with the palette knife, with the addition of a few drops of oil. If the white is made soft and manageable, all the colors of the palette mixed with it will be so. White, we discover, is the medium for oil painting, serving the same purpose as the whiteness of the canvas in the stain, or of the paper in water color. The luminosity of some color, as the flesh tints in Renoir's nudes, is attained by permitting the white canvas to shine through the transparent pigment. The glistening sunshine or sunlight effects in other paintings, such as Monet's cathedrals and meadows, is attained by mixing great quantities of white into all the colors. The technique is necessarily impasto (put on thick, as a paste); the picture is pitched high in key. Gauguin's paintings are accomplished with a minimum of white and are consequently rich in intensity of color as well as low in key.

We begin approximating the colors of the stain. The yellow of the bowl is the same zinc yellow (with the addition of a bit of white in place of the thinned-out pure yellow). The green remains the same in the dark areas and the lighter green is matched by adding zinc white. The cover of the book, instead of being an incandescent orange, is painted with vermilion, a bit of white and a touch of blue. The light edge of the book is put down as almost pure white, the shadow edge is painted with alizarin and blue mixed with white to a violet and then covered by a stroke or two of yellow orange mixed with white. So far this is our first experience in the mixing of gray. (The many ways of making neutral colors

will be considered in the next chapter.) Of course gray may
be made from black and white very quickly, but such a gray
is apt to lack the special quality of a light surface in shadow.
The reflections caught by a thing in shadow, the way in
which the local color of the object seems to penetrate the
shadow, the quality of luminosity in shadows, all these conditions preclude the use of an opaque, flat gray such as that
made by black and white. For this reason black is, for the
time being, excluded from our palette.

Now we attempt to give interest to the study in two ways,
pattern and form. We seek out variations in the folds and
shadows of the background and foreground and use them to
divide the otherwise monotonous areas. Then we turn our
attention to the form of the individual objects. In the case
of the book, which is made by three flat planes, there is little
we can do to intensify its tactile sensation. With the little
pitcher and the yellow bowl, however, the effect of roundness and volume is of the highest importance. Attaining this
effect will be largely the measure of the success of the study.
From a technical point of view this task is the most difficult
one for the novice. Where the charcoal study expresses volume through the use of planes of light and planes of dark,
the painting must translate these values into color values.

Each dark plane, examined carefully for color, appears to
have a special hue, or nuance. It is not only darker than the
light plane next to it but is also colder (more to the blue)
or warmer (more orange). The variations of color *model*
the object, that is, give it tactile value, quite as much as do
the gradations of dark (value) themselves. Previous to
Cezanne the painter made a round object appear round by
value alone, that is, by using one color in gradations just as
we have used the charcoal. But Cezanne demonstrated how

the juxtaposition of planes in alternate sequence, warm and cool, give far greater tactile value. The problem before the student is to take the flat color value arrived at by his stain and give it form through planes of color, some warm, some cool, the hues of which he must determine by his own eyes. To clarify the nature of this problem we reproduce the two stages of the painting, the stain (Plate II*a*) and an object in the completed picture (Plate II*b*).

PLATE II*a*.—The stain

PLATE II*b*.—An object painted in planes

V

NOTES ON COLOR AND OTHER MATTERS

THE FIRST work of the amateur painter will fill him with mixed emotions. While the thrill of accomplishment will be experienced, it may be mitigated by doubts and dissatisfactions. "Yes, I made it all myself," he may say. "It really looks like something in nature. But this object has no volume. It seems distorted. The color is muddy in spots and as a matter of fact it looks a little messy generally. Still it's something to have done all alone."

Bad color generally results from timidity. It is better to have the color wrong than to attempt to correct it by scumbling. Scumbling is the process (or rather the habit) of rubbing a thin bit of pigment over a color in a last minute effort to modify it. The result is a last minute haze which modifies the color to the point of extinction. All that remains is the tint. Weak color is frequently traceable to the stain; if the color relations are too subtle in the first statement, the finished picture will appear hazy and fail to carry.

The first study is apt to suffer from two other common defects, chalkiness and acidity. A chalky picture is one in which there is a preponderance of white in the pigment so that every passage of color will have the same quality. Pigments have their own properties; a yellow has luminosity, a blue, depth. When these properties are lost in an excessive amount of white, a chalky study results.

An acid picture, on the other hand, results frequently from

failure to use white in sufficient quantities. A picture in which the colors have the harsh intensity of dyes, particularly the cold colors, is as uninteresting as a chalky one. Examples of acid colors are magenta and chartreuse.

It is often difficult to determine whether a color is cold or warm. This should not disturb the student as colors, with very definite exceptions, are warm and cool only in a relative, not an absolute sense. On the palette the color may appear one way, in the study another.

At the end of this chapter some combinations will be suggested for attaining certain less decided, neutral colors. Even after the student has had much practice in these combinations, he will be at a loss to express such colors when they appear in objects under special conditions of lighting. A simple way then of reaching the effect is to resolve the color into its nearest secondary color. For example, a gray may be made a violet; a brown a purple or green. Thus if an object is a gray bowl, it may first be painted a clean violet and then altered by an overpainting of its opposite color, warm yellow, to the desired gray; or the reverse, depending upon whether the cool or the warm is dominant in the gray.

The ability to mix grays of either warm or cool hues must be cultivated if overstatement, harshness, and excessive sweetness of color are to be avoided. The key to this is the knowledge of opposite or complementary colors. Any pair of complementaries will result in gray, although each combination will produce a slightly different result since pigments are not absolutely pure in color. The color wheel below (Figure 6) shows which are the complementaries.

Of the above combinations the most useful will probably be the orange and cobalt, particularly for light values where transparency is desired. There is, however, a rule to observe carefully when using pigments which are in themselves un-equal in value. Before two colors are combined, they should be made equal in value by the addition of white to the darker color. The orange is several shades lighter than the cobalt; the cobalt should therefore be brought to the value of the orange by the addition of white before combining with it. Otherwise there will not be a clean fusion. Grays made from this combination will be either warm or cool depending upon which pigment is made to dominate the other.

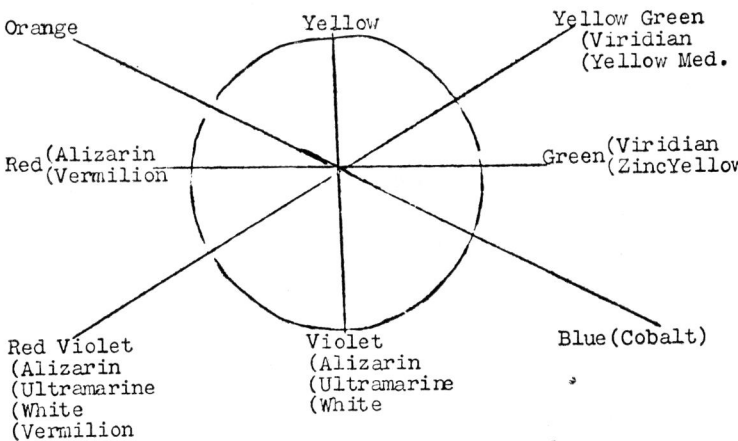

FIGURE 6.—The complementary colors

A useful combination which is not made of exact comple-mentaries is alizarin and viridian. The color resulting from this mixture will appear black. When white is added to it in various quantities, cool pearly grays are attained which are very different in quality from the orange-cobalt mixture. They are more metallic, less luminous grays.

Brown is another color difficult to control. Theoretically it is made of red, yellow, and blue. Mix these together and the result will be surprisingly muddy. But if you make two batches of secondary colors which complement each other and impose one upon the other, a fine rich brown will result. This of course will only be one of a number of hues of brown. Some browns are transparent; some luminous, like whisky seen against the light; some opaque, like chocolate. A useful exercise in making browns is as follows: With the palette knife mix a batch of alizarin and ultramarine to a purple, then add orange. Spread the resulting brown in two directions. On one side alter the color in small patches by the addition of a little vermilion, then yellow medium, then zinc yellow. On the other do the same with cobalt and viridian. All the colors so obtained will be either luminous or intense. Now if white is added to each, not only will they be made lighter but their characters will be definitely changed. They will become opaque and slightly grayed.

Shadows, because of their warmth and coolness, grayness and brownness, are always troublesome to the amateur still-life painter. When the student comes to paint outdoors, he will discover that sunlight turns every color warm and that shadows, except when reflecting neighboring surfaces, are cold. This is the reverse of conditions indoors where the light source is the north sky. Under such light the shadows are often warm, the local color determining any question. But the light, again except where reflected, is cold and bluish so that even upon the warmest orange object the principal spot of light will have in it more than a touch of blue. It is interesting to note that the success of moonlight scenes depends largely on this indoor color system because moonlight is more like north light than like sunlight.

The dramatic quality of those paintings which we call Romantic is due largely to the treatment of shadows. Shadows evoke imaginative thought and stir our emotions. Perhaps this is because they are associated in our consciousness with childhood fears and adventures. Whether this be the reason or not, the picture with soft and mysterious shadows intrigues us more than the one in which the shadows are sharp, brilliant, and flat. A certain suggestibility is imparted to shadows by making the objects emerge from them instead of merely juxtaposing object and shadow. The contour of an object may be cut out sharply in light on one side and be lost entirely on the other. The object then appears to have volume, to grow out of the background. Much of Rembrandt's dramatic power can be attributed to his phenomenal skill in making forms emerge into the light. Study of his means will reveal the importance of suppression of contour on the shadow side.

Since so many still-life subjects are round vessels having ellipses, the novice is often in doubt as to how to make them appear openings instead of blocks of color. When openings or mouths of objects appear to be a sharp black they may be painted a dark purple blue (alizarin and ultramarine). If this is too harsh for the surrounding colors, it may be softened and warmed by the addition of a very little orange or orange-green. The opposition of the two colors will give the opening depth. A similar procedure is useful in the painting of cast shadows, particularly those made by electric light. However, too rigid an observance of formula results in monotonous painting. There is much pleasure to be derived from studying nuances of shadows. And no exercise will better train the student in the manipulation of neutral colors. Note: In passing one color over another remember to have both of approximately the same value.

The painting of folds of drapery in background and foreground is perhaps the most difficult technical feat for the still-life painter. Not only must the drapery be arranged for pattern, but its texture must be considered if it is to be made to look like material other than wood. On the other hand, there are many excellent painters who are so overcome with the textural quality of shimmering materials that they sacrifice all softness and form to the metallic sheen. The serious painter is concerned first of all with the form under the material, then with the tactile value of the cloth or covering. He attempts to convey not only the effect of light on a dazzling surface but the feeling of roundness and air in each fold. His brush strokes will reflect this concern. Instead of making a clever sweeping stroke for the light plane and another for the shadow of the fold, he will build the entire fold in planes, using the brush *across* the fold instead of in the direction of the fold. One evidence of Cezanne's untiring search for the foundations of appearances is to be found in his method of painting a limp towel or tablecloth. He does not suggest; he states with certainty this is how it lies, this is where it is creased, and that is where it humps up in a tubular fold. Sculptural form with him always took precedence over clever suggestion.

Every student, and artist too, is annoyed by the tricks played by pigment in its oxidization. A passage will be painted in clear and forceful, and when the painter returns to it after an interval of several days, it will appear to have vanished in a fog. Sometimes this is due to working over color that is not sufficiently dry. Sometimes it is due to the composition of the pigment. If the color is poorly ground, the linseed oil will be absorbed and the color sink in, or become "matt." Poor grades of canvas board also cause this condition, the covering permitting the oil to soak into the paper base. The only thing to do is to restore the painted passage temporarily so that progress with the rest of the canvas will not be delayed. A very soft sable brush moistened with damar varnish or commercial retouch varnish may be passed lightly over the matt parts of the study. Be sure the brush is thoroughly dry as dampness will cause the varnish to turn milky on the canvas. The best retouch varnish is a French product (Vibert) popular with painters for many decades. It is a solution of damar varnish in petroleum distillates. If used according to directions it will restore the freshness of the painting and preserve it until permanent varnishing, some six months later. Complete oxidization of commercial pigment requires from six months to a year. At that time a clear mastic varnish, thinned a little with turpentine, may be used to protect the painted surface.

It sometimes happens that the sunken part of the picture was not completed, or that it is necessary to add detail. In that case it will be unsatisfactory to restore the original color and values in the above manner and then to proceed with embellishment or added detail. The only satisfactory course is to repaint the entire passage. Before repainting, however, the safest procedure is to scrape that part of the canvas with the palette knife, removing as much of the pigment as possible without destroying the texture of the canvas. If one proceeds in this way the completed picture is more apt to be free from the jarring distortion of values and the weak, smoky effects so unaccountable to the beginner.

The manner of applying paint is not the important consideration today that it was when academic art ruled the cultural roost. At that time instruction was principally concerned with technique. The instructor took the brush, poised it, and with a subtle turn of the wrist and the proper pressure upon the canvas made a few masterly strokes which created a nose upon a portrait. The student strained his perceptions to acquire that deftness. When he passed into other classes he became subject to other mannerisms in the application of paint. Art was truly the clever performance.

Today it is not how you say it; it is what you say. The

important objective is to get clean color instead of uncertain, weak fumblings. Beyond this any means are acceptable. The paint may be applied with palette knife in various ways. It may be smoothed with cloths or fingers, scratched with sharp points, kept thin or thick. Any technique which results in a sharp, definite statement, strong in its color relations and pattern, is satisfactory.

The foregoing should enable the reader to overcome most of the difficulties experienced in the first study. The second study like the first should be limited to three objects and two or three areas for background. While the color generally should be restricted to primary and secondary colors, the forms of the objects may be a little more involved. Fruits and vegetables offer a great variety of colors and forms. A green pepper, for example, or a bunch of carrots, will make an interesting exercise. The forms of bottles are always good material for study, particularly when they are decorated with attractive labels. Such homely things as the blue electric bulb and the carton in which it is packed also are good for still-life study.

As command of the palette grows, the amateur may experiment with objects of tertiary or neutral color, or of slightly grayed primary and secondary colors. The grayed yellow of a ripe banana, the blackish purple of an egg plant, the silvery warm and cool grays fused into the color of an aluminum cooking utensil, the terra cotta flower pot, the copper kettle, all offer a challenge to the inexperienced painter. Much struggling with such complicated colors may be avoided by the practice of making color charts before beginning the painting. The exercise below is an example of such a chart.

Exercise: On a canvas board 12″ x 16″ ruled into one inch squares paint the following:

1. *Deep red to yellowish pink:*

a. alizarin
   vermilion

b. alizarin
   orange

c. alizarin
   orange
   zinc yellow

d. alizarin
   orange
   white

e. vermilion
   zinc yellow
   white

f. vermilion
   zinc yellow
   white
   cobalt

2. *Greens*

a. viridian
   white

b. viridian
   zinc yellow

c. viridian
   yellow med.

d. viridian
   yellow med.
   orange

e. viridian
   orange
   white

f. viridian
   white
   cobalt

g. ultramarine
   zinc yellow

h. ultramarine
   yellow med.

3. *Violets*

a. alizarin
   ultramarine
   white

b. alizarin
   ultramarine
   white
   vermilion

c. alizarin
   ultramarine
   white
   cobalt

d. alizarin
   ultramarine
   white
   zinc yellow

e. alizarin
   ultramarine
   white
   viridian

Make the following colors as suggested:

Olive green—viridian, orange and white.

Gray violet—alizarin, ultramarine and viridian and white.

Grayed salmon pink—vermilion, zinc yellow, cobalt and white.

Yellow brown—brown plus additional viridian, yellow medium and orange.

Brick red—alizarin, vermilion, yellow-green and white.

Black—alizarin, ultramarine and viridian.

In summing up these notes on color a few rules are here listed:

1. In combining two batches of mixed colors to obtain a third, see that both batches are of approximately the same value.

2. Dirty brushes (or palette knife) cannot give the desired color. Keep one brush for yellow, one for orange and red, one for blue and violet, one for green, and one for brown and gray. Occasionally rinse all brushes in clean turpentine. When a brush picks up a foreign color, clean it carefully before proceeding.

3. To alter a color, do not apply pigment to a wet surface. First remove original color carefully by scraping and washing.

4. Keep pigment to the consistency of paste. Do not thin it excessively with oil.

5. Keep the palette workable. Clean it from time to time. Do not use pigment accidentally polluted by other pigment. The palette should at all times present a neat appearance.

After a winter of still-life study the student may venture to paint on linen canvas. One objection to boards has already been mentioned—the tendency to absorb the oil in which the pigment is ground because of the poor grade of covering and the capillary action of the paper base. Another objection to boards is that they become warped (and expensive) as they increase in size. Canvas escapes these faults. Its great advantage, however, is the resiliency of its surface; it responds more readily, takes the paint more easily, permits a more varied treatment. A good size for a start is 16″ x 20″. A yard of canvas 44″ wide (price $1.75 for ordinary linen) will make four coverings. The stretcher strips which are mortised for quick and accurate assembling are priced at about twenty-five cents for a set of four. Buy your first canvas already stretched, observe how it is done, and from then on cover your own.

Still life will always afford excellent study regardless of the type of painting you hope ultimately to do. Progress will be most rapid where the study is regarded only as such and not as a picture. Resist the natural urge to "finish" the exercise, the ambition to produce large canvases with involved arrangements of many objects, the impulse to imitate styles seen in exhibitions. Paint much but not on one work —at least not until you have acquired some knowledge of composition from the exercises later suggested.

VI

INTRODUCTION TO STILL LIFE AS ART

As THE "studio" becomes profusely ornamented with still-life studies, increasingly interesting in color and arrangement, the amateur will experience a new pleasure. The fun of doing the thing will have passed. But it will have left in its place not just the souvenir, but the satisfaction of seeing the projection, however slight, of one's personality. In all likelihood the proud novitiate is already patronizing the frame makers, selecting machined and fussy mouldings with which to embellish his simple studies.

It may be unkind therefore (but in the nature of a duty) to interrupt the mood of pride and satisfaction by recalling the admonition given earlier regarding the rôle assigned to the amateur. The unrestrained praise of wife and friends does sometimes work havoc with the part-time painter. He should beware the thought that he is mysteriously linked in spirit to Paul Gauguin. His painting may be neat, it may even be competent, but the chances are it is not art. Art is not the product of rules and principles; it is the thing which restates rules and principles according to the demands of its maker's personality. The personality of the artist is not, of course, that outward quality of behavior associated with charm and salesmanship; it finds its expression only in the work.

The precise nature of the artist's personality is the subject of many imposing treatises and need not here be considered. Suffice it to say that the theories expounded stress the indi

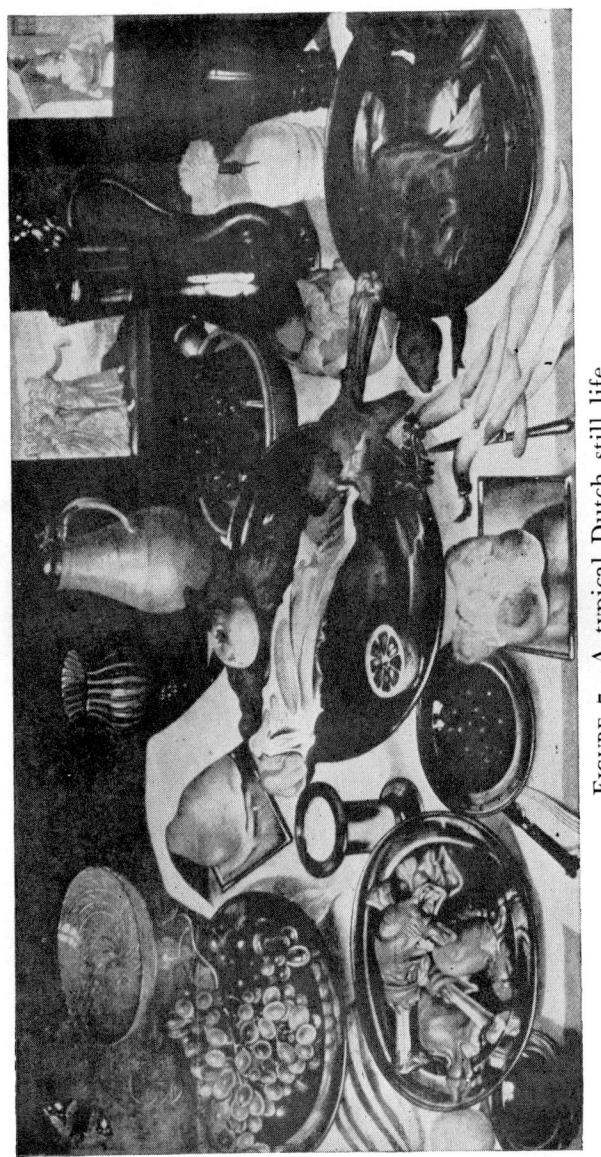

FIGURE 7.—A typical Dutch still life

FIGURE 8.—*Still Life* by Chardin (1699-1779)

vidual, or unique, or abnormal character of the artist. The essential fact for us is that with all his freedom from restraint the artist expresses himself in a circumscribed art-form, yet conveys something beyond the demands of that form, something hitherto unexpressed. The ordinary man will approach art through knowledge, intelligence, command of the art-form—yet will not attain it. The work of art cannot be produced merely through these capacities or ingredients. The necessary leaven is a personality beyond the estimable normal.

The amateur painter need not for this reason abandon painting. Art is not merely beauty. Art is something beautiful which lives while mere beauty vanishes. Yet it is mere beauty which is an important substance of our lives. Beauty is order, competence, perfection. We may all at times achieve this. To reduce this matter of beauty and art to practical application it may be said that the business of the amateur painter is to make something beautiful (however perishable) while the business of the artist is to revise notions of beauty, for by so doing he keeps alive and stimulates the very sensibility to beauty.

All this is in the nature of an introduction to a view of three paintings of still life which are unquestionably competent and which are considered art by many cultured and educated people. The first picture is a sixteenth century still life by an unknown Dutch painter (Figure 7). The Dutch were, like the earlier Venetians, principally *genre* painters; that is, their aim in art was to record the everyday incidents of middle-class life. Such painting has for subject matter public events, ceremonies, feasts, intimate family scenes, the interior of the home, and still life. But while the Venetians (notably Gentile Bellini and Carpaccio) made beautiful designs and compositions of massed figures and seemed concerned above all with showing human dignity, the Dutch and Flemish painters of genre often sacrificed both dignity and design to the jolly story. It was a social and esthetic precept that their pictures (excepting religious subjects) express a pleasant mood, sometimes a gay and boisterous mood, but always a hallelujah for the good life. (Breughel, it is true, was the equal of any Venetian in the art of composition. And the genre painting of Vermeer stands so far above typical Dutch painting that he appears to be using the Dutch idiom to express the finest Venetian humanism. The Dutch and Flemish schools of genre, however, are far behind these two geniuses.)

Still-life painting, then, is a Dutch subject matter. The artist put before the spectator a list of appetizing dishes that were customar'ly found on the festive boards of the period and bade him feast—his eyes.

In the picture reproduced we see the whole *table d'hote* set out at once. It is not so much a picture as a list of pictured objects. Our interest is not at all in the relative positions of the objects. There is no grouping, no pattern. There are only things to eat and their containers. If the actual painting of these things were not distinguished by an almost uncanny execution which amazes us by its realism, the canvas would be a pictograph rather than a picture.

To make clear how dependent the painting is upon its one esthetic quality, craftsmanship, let us imagine the objects painted in a merely photographic technique—minutely rendered and impeccable. Our glance identifies, reads, and passes on. After looking over the canvas twice we ask ourselves with the concern of a waiter, "Have we missed anything?" and then satisfied that all has been taken in, we put an abrupt end to our interest in the painting. It is the technical skill in reproducing the accidental appearances of things which holds our attention and interest. It is obvious that in the days before the camera was dreamed of, such skill in reporting surface appearances would be regarded a much greater esthetic accomplishment and objective than it is today.

In this machine age mere surface realism painted by hand is utterly without esthetic meaning. Correct or realistic reporting is left to the photographer. If we know anything at all about the art of painting, we do not in looking at a still life ask, "Is that grape, in your opinion, one of those seedless very sweet varieties?" or "Is that object cast aluminum or just an alloy?" We ask for a different kind of description; we demand other effects and results from painting. We question whether the artist has made us feel the nature of the thing by an intensification of its physical reality (not realism), its volume, its weight, its peculiar and particular combination of forms. And more important even than this, we demand that the thing be made part of a collection of objects which, through their differences and relations, offset each other while impinging on each other. In the words of the painter, we demand a rhythm which results from interval, direction, linear design, volume and space—the elements of composition. (We shall investigate each in order in later chapters.) The Dutch still life lacks all of these plastic elements. (Color is also a vital element of composition but since the reproduction is in black and white we must overlook it.)

Passing from the extravagant display of a dinerless dinner by a Dutch master to a still life by Chardin (Figure 8) is in its first effect like reaching the quiet of your apartment after a strenuous and giddy day of Christmas shopping. Chardin is the poet of quietude, of modest pleasures, and delight in humble things.

To make poetry of ordinary things taxes the gifts of the great artist. If you can paint images of seductive nudes and enormous murals of crowds, you need not be a great master to impress people with your worthiness. The subject matter will floor the spectator, who will attribute the effect to your genius rather than to his own primary interest in the things depicted. The easel painting, the small still life, depends more exactly upon the qualities in its painting, and unfortunately a knowledge of these qualities is not too prevalent. The megalomania which has affected America's architecture is now affecting its painting. If the easel picture goes out of fashion, it will be because of a general decline of esthetic standards, since no other form of painting is more exacting, or when capably done, more charged with plastic poetry.

The argument has been put forth that just as the camera has rendered Dutch genre obsolete, so the machine age has doomed the easel picture to extinction. This is a confused notion. As long as man retains his physical dimensions and dwells in interiors commensurate with these proportions (from the point of view of comfort and efficiency), so long will he feel the need of small pictures. Until his eyes evolve to the size of automobile headlights, he will be incapable of seeing completely an enormous painting, except in fragmentary or in distant views. The mental notion of machine influence on the other hand will affect the *treatment* of the painting. The picture will not be as large as a machine shop but will be painted in plastic forms resembling to an extent those of machinery.

In this connection it is interesting to note that one of the greatest of painters of small still-life studies, the above mentioned Chardin, lived in an age given over completely to the fluff and glamour of courtly romanticism—of large and flamboyant pictures. The habits and fashions of the Regency had no effect upon his art. He had seen Dutch still life and felt it lacking. His aim was to give esthetic meaning to homely things. Removed from the time and the public taste he cultivated a classical simplicity.

Studying the reproduction of Chardin's still life, the first quality we note is order. No conflicting tensions disturb the serenity of the arrangement. Serenity is imparted by the long horizontal strip of the foreground and the placid vertical to the left. (A placid world is flat and upright, horizontal and vertical; a chaotic or dramatic world is made by diagonals. This is a simple psychological device of the painter. In the chapters dealing with composition we shall see a further use of direction as a maker of moods.) There is only one diagonal, the stem of the pipe, and it serves to break the monotony of the arrangement. A second one would jar the mood of the picture. Note first the division of area—the different widths of horizontal and vertical strips along the two edges, the light pattern of the foreground which builds up in the mass of the pitcher. The ear or handle of the pitcher introduces another shape and carries the light back to the surface of the table. See how the pitcher is placed—not in the center of the canvas, nor too far to one side. And observe the way the small bowl and cover are grouped at its base. Added interest in the arrangement is given by the placing of other objects at unequal intervals from the important pitcher-group. These minor objects (or themes) are connected to the major group by the diagonal pipe stem on the left and the fold of cloth on the right at the base of the goblet. The dark chest in the background gives further variety of pattern and expands the range of value of the whole study.

This rough analysis is made for the purpose of indicating the reasons for the orderliness or organization of the picture.

But it is not to be assumed that orderly quiet is the sum of Chardin's art; it is only a requisite, a condition to the expression of his other qualities. The tones of a violin cannot be heard in the din of a garage; the instrument must be played in a place of perfect quiet. And so it is with Chardin's art. The subtlety of his handling of pigment would be meaningless in such an unresolved and noisy composition as the Dutch still life. But having established order he proceeds to extract every bit of melody from the light, the shadow, the surface texture of each object. He loses edges, plays with the tantalizing warmth and coolness of shadows, rolls the pigment in little lumps and piles it on to capture the feel of clay. The variety of his handling shows his serious determined effort to give the material of objects as well as their shape and volume and color. And so the spectator has the sensation of looking at something true and real and permanent. It is not a collection of things to make the mouth water. It is not a clever photograph made from novel camera angles with ingenious lighting effects. It is an artist's attempt to extract the utmost reality from things in nature while endowing them with the charm of his own personality.

Chardin's art has remained through the centuries as a sort of resting place for artists tired of the politics of painting. Pious Classicist and ardent Romanticist have alike found pleasure in his quiet esthetic. But while his name has been a byword in studios for generations, the public has not been made sufficiently aware of his importance in the history of art. Not until a crude convert to Impressionism repeated Chardin's faculty for organizing plain things into pictures did critics rediscover the eighteenth century master. This Impressionist who was a devout respecter of Chardin's simple art was the Provençal Frenchman, Paul Cezanne.

The theory and program of Impressionism was touched

upon in an earlier chapter. The philosophy underlying it has filled many books and will fill many more. For our purpose it is enough to know that the fresh clean color in pictures and in decoration which we have taken for granted all our lives is a comparatively recent discovery of Impressionism. We have only to wander through museums to see how limited in color were the old masters. Everything is brown, blue-green or rose-red—mostly brown. It was the brilliant hues and colors of the prism which suggested the theory that light is composed of all colors like a rainbow. And that except for those definite dividing places, red, yellow, and blue, all colors were composed of atoms of these pure colors. It was natural that painters convinced of the scientific importance of this doctrine should demand a new palette—that is, a new set of colors. The earth colors, the brick reds, the olive greens, the clay yellows, and murky browns, were all discarded. Purity of color was of prime importance and experiment led to the selection of crimson, vermilion, the cadmiums, the cobalts, ultramarine, and emeraude. Certain other colors, as for instance emerald green, pure and beautiful in their tubes, were found to be fugitive and were abandoned. Regardless then of the theory of color atoms and their combination, a real and momentous change in the art of painting was brought about by the new palette of the Impressionists.

Paul Cezanne was a convert to this new color usage. The purity and vibration of it may have enchanted him, but the philosophy underlying it was antipathetic to his nature. Whoever has seen Impressionist pictures knows that their hazy tonality fuses the objects, flattens out the forms, and destroys both the sense of volume and the sense of space. To this destruction of Classic Greek esthetic precepts Cezanne objected. The problem then was how to paint volume and space in the vibrational color of Impressionism. He solved this problem by making planes of contrasting color—instead of spots of color—vibrate.

While this technical discovery may have passed into history and into the classrooms of art schools, there is something in the discoverer's pictures which belongs only to him. There is a quality of sincerity that overwhelms the facile painter. There is an intelligence in organization which is common only to great masters. Finally there is poetry in the choice of subject matter and the handling of it. For these reasons Cezanne recalls the name of Chardin, and the name of Chardin brings up that of Cezanne.

Since our interest in Cezanne's art is here limited to his manner of presentation, we shall for the time being pass over his important contribution to color usage (the subject of a subsequent chapter). In the still life reproduced (Figure 9) the pattern is almost a silhouette of white against dark. Within each large pattern, however, there are interesting minor patterns or divisions of space. This is as true of the white cloth as it is of the decorative materials in the background. The fruit likewise is grouped into patterns. Even the solitary apple in the center is related to the other apples, putting a halt to the circular movement of the eye from group to group. It also establishes a point from which every form radiates. Every square inch of the canvas is used and is necessary for the balance of the arrangement. The forms grow out of each other.

Note for example the oval at the bottom of the table cloth, right side. It is modeled independently as if it were a section of metal pipe. But the fold within this form leads us out of it and back into other lines and forms. The entire cloth is a study in articulation of volumes held in relation by interesting line.

This element of line is what I want particularly to call to

the attention of the student. The basis of abstraction is to be found in the design of forms in Cezanne's art. The forms are given definition through the geometrical line. As few modernists excel Cezanne in inventiveness in variation of line, we are going to an immediate source of abstract art in studying this example. Observe first the variations in contour of cloth, fruit bowl, and pitcher. Then note the opposition of the lines which occur within each part of the contour. Or follow the series of lines below the single apple. There are five or six lines each different in character. The effectiveness of wavy or scalloped lines is dependent upon the opposition of simple geometrical lines. Rhythms are created by repetitions. A study of this line relationship and opposition, done with the charcoal point, and accenting the more important lines with smudge, will be a most fruitful investigation for the beginner.

It will be of little use to the student to widen the chasm between mere seeing and actual doing. We must therefore interrupt our excursion along the road of still-life art. There have been many developments in this art since Cezanne. But because they involve the art of composition which we have hardly more than touched upon and moreover rest upon new esthetic objectives, we had better retrace our steps and renew our acquaintance with the paint box.

Exercise: Using a still-life study already painted as a basis, and without greatly altering the relative positions of the objects, arrange a composition in which the pattern is attained by severe geometrical line. Plate III illustrates the objective.

VII

THE OUTDOOR SKETCH

A WINTER'S experience in still-life painting will be sufficient to make the amateur acquainted with the paint box.
Still life may not be the easiest branch of the art, but at
least it offers a fairly stable model for the painter unless the
fruit in his set-up goes bad. But generally it can be counted
upon not to move its position or change its color, and so the
beginner is relieved of bothersome instability while he is
struggling with elementary color.

Many students of painting become initiated into the craft
by sketching out-of-doors. But landscape is hardly desirable
as a first steppingstone. The rapid changes of nature tax the
resources of even the experienced artist, and the groping
beginner can hardly find pleasure in the losing struggle. He
too often falls into mannerisms and forced effects in default
of a competent method of recording the scene before him.
Yet no kind of painting affords more enjoyment than outdoor
sketching if the painter can work rapidly and with some degree of assurance. For such the coming of Spring will offer
a double enjoyment, the painting adventure and the outdoor
activity.

To those going out to paint landscape for the first time a
few words of advice and caution will be helpful. The indoor
painter will have fallen unconsciously into a gamut of values
and range of color termed a key. The indoor key is comparatively low. Out in the open it will be unsuitable. The

PLATE III.—Geometrical pattern in the still life

higher key required can be attained simply by the addition of white (and possibly yellow) to almost all the colors, and a studied avoidance of the deep neutral darks employed for indoor shadows. *Coolness* will take the place of darkness. By this transference no violation of value will occur, but the study will be pitched in a higher key. Closely related to the high key is the matter of cleanliness in brush and pigment. Indoors a slurred stroke will give that grayness which envelops and unifies objects. But outdoors the same grayish tone will kill the atmospheric brilliance, and too often result in a dirty picture. Dirtiness of color is ever the bane of the novice painter; out-of-doors it is apt to conquer him unless he observe closely the rule that the brush be wiped after every stroke. (It need hardly be mentioned at this stage that separate brushes be used for each decided color.) Even when painting an area of one color the brush should be repeatedly wiped and loaded afresh with clean pigment. Frequent brushing over one spot may result in dullness or muddiness caused by the careless picking up of juxtaposed color. In other words, no niggling is permissible; each stroke must be calculated and decisively applied. Dry, rather than fluid, pigment will enable the student to achieve a clean, bright sketch.

Before attacking the mechanics of outdoor sketching it will be profitable to consider certain esthetic requirements of the successful sketch. The subject selected should have as great a variety of colored areas as possible. By this is not meant a variety of spots of color as in a mountainside in Autumn, but a scene in which there are natural divisions or patterns of color made by trees, meadows, buildings, clouds; by sunlight and shadow, by darks and lights. Such an assemblage of patterns will not only make an interesting sketch, but what is more important, will develop the student's sense of design, and give him the valuable experience of relating colors properly. The amateur's usual response to the beauties of nature, a monotonous sea of green, is not only bad painting, but an avoidance of the exercise in color-relating essential to the painter's development.

It is to be kept in mind that the outdoor sketch is not the same thing as the landscape painting. On this theme more will be said in the section devoted to composition, but here arises one point pertinent to the selection of subject matter. The landscape picture may be a panorama or a whole novelette as in the eighteenth and early nineteenth century English paintings. The sketch is theoretically only notebook material for the painter to consult. Actually a sketch may have more charm and esthetic value than a finished landscape of an area covering ten square miles. But the limitations of the sketch are positive. It records at most a two-hour interval in the day and it comprises only those essentials which can be recorded in that working period. The sketch therefore should either be a close-up of a colorful spot such as a corner of a barnyard, a clump of trees by a pool, a wharf, a street of buildings, etc.,—in all of which the sharp color relations should be apparent—or else it should in the broadest terms state the particular time of day of the landscape by means of simple areas of color. The latter intention should be left to the experienced painter since it is a much more exacting kind of painting requiring swift and sure statement of oftentimes subtle hues and nuances.

Aside from the ever-present difficulty of keeping the sketch clean, the two most arresting problems of the student will be the painting of foliage and the handling of sunlight and shadow. The Impressionists used to say, "Paint the foliage in an airy way, loose and leafy, so that a bird could fly through it," and pointed to Corot's delicate treatment invented long before Impressionism. For a picture composed of atmosphere and jeweled spots this is useful admonition. But for our present-day robust notions of volume and space it means nothing. Rather should it be said, "Paint the tree in such a way that it will stand in distinct and proper relation spatially to other trees about it. Separate it from the others and likewise separate its masses of foliage one from the other, giving volume to each." To do this properly will require three observances. First, the various trees must be given definite shapes. Second, each shape must be given a quality of color unlike the others. Third, the modeling of each mass of foliage, by means of planes of light and dark (exactly as in still life) should be subordinated to the volume of the tree as a whole. Cezanne's paintings illustrate this point. Trees painted with regard for the spatial relation and the weight and bulk of their masses of foliage will convey a sense of reality which no photograph could possibly give. The trees will be what Berenson calls "architectonic," giving us the illusion of mass at a precise distance from other masses or objects and covering a certain area. Without some *a priori* method such as this the sketch is too likely to result in a smudgy, cottony green fantasy.

The tendency of the novice is to paint all foliage with emeraude green or viridian, lightened by white or zinc yellow. No color requires as much diversity in hue and quality as green. (Hue means the cast of the color, its particular affinity for another color. Quality means its degree of transparence, opaqueness, intensity, dullness, incandescence, mattness, oiliness, etc.) Theoretically, green is a mixture of blue and yellow. The combinations then are almost limitless, each resulting in an individuality subtle or strong. The table below (essentially a restatement of the color exercise) will suggest a few of these combinations.

Ultramarine and zinc yellow
Ultramarine and cadmium yellow pale
Ultramarine and cadmium yellow medium
Ultramarine and cadmium orange
Ultramarine and viridian or emeraude

Cobalt blue used in place of ultramarine will vary all the above combinations.

Viridian or emeraude mixed with zinc yellow and the cadmiums will give the most brilliant and intense greens. A warm green of great luminosity is made of orange and emeraude. This may be converted into a soft, deep, warm green by the admixture of a bit of alizarin or vermilion.

All these greens are variable, of course, depending on proportion of mixtures and on value (degree of light determined by the amount of white or light yellow added).

In addition to the above combinations there are many beautiful and odd gray-greens made by the mixing of earth colors and other blues and even by the use of black. These we shall investigate in the chapter "Expanding the Palette."

Considerable practice will be necessary before the student will be able to bring a green landscape to life. Fumbling may be avoided by the preparation of a chart of squares of as many different combinations as possible, each labeled. The chart should be divided into warm greens and cool greens. It is curious that most of the poor landscape studies of beginners are marked by excessive acidity (zinc yellow and emeraude) and excessive coldness (blue) of the greens. However, warm greens when applied haphazardly are apt to pass into murky browns.

The matter of warmth and coolness of color is related to the problem of sunlight and shadow; is indeed often the same problem, for sunlight is generally warm and shadows cool—

the reverse of conditions indoors where light (north light or sky light) is cool and shadows usually warm. The indoor condition is approached out-of-doors on gray days where the dominant light is sky rather than sun. This does not mean that the landscape on a gray day should be treated by formula, that the top foliage on a golden tree should be painted a cool brassy color, or a dim shadow cast by a building be rendered by an expanse of hot brown. The principle is given only as an aid in determining the nature of the color seen. It is only in bright moonlight that it may be entirely relied upon, as many indoor moonlight artists have demonstrated.

In sunlight the changes from local color are drastic. We find the shadows of green foliage transformed to deep blue and violet, the lights intensely yellow. Here again the principle of yellowish sunlight and blue shadow is apt to be turned into a tiresome formula. As a preventive against a banal application of the rule there are two resorts, brilliant exaggeration in flat pattern so that interest is captured by the novel design, or such subtlety as results in no two areas being precisely of the same hue or quality of color. The latter will prove the more profitable path for the learner, though naturally the more difficult.

Finesse is to be attained as much through imagination as through patience and plodding care. In catching elusive and subtle color the first requisite is a bold and venturesome spirit. The timid painter will try effects upon his palette, forgetful of the fact that true color is true only in relation to the color surrounding it. While the bold painter will place one color upon another on his canvas, modifying it to its proper hue, the timid painter must be assured that the color he is looking at is made by this, that and the other pigment all mixed together on the palette. And so he will spend much of his time fumbling for the correct combination. Such a method or attitude will take all the joy out of painting for there is no final answer in color, only a proper or false relationship. What color, for example, is black in sunlight? How should the side of an unpainted barn in shadow be rendered—the shingles on the roof, gray and weather-stained, yet glowing in the afternoon sun? Or a concrete wall in shadow? These things are resolved by different painters in different ways.

One method is to divide the picture into its two divisions of sunlight and shadow, painting the one in a thin oily buff color and the other in a thin oily violet. The local color is then worked into each part until an approximation of the actual scene is reached. The disadvantage of this method is that it results too often in a monotonous and weakly colored design in yellow and blue. The opposite method is to paint all objects in their local color as they would appear on a gray day and then to impose sunlight and shadow as required. This method usually results in murky color and darkness. The first method would be satisfactory if the use of oil and white as a medium were avoided.

A turpentine wash or stain restricted (as in still life) to a few blatant notes, yellow, orange, violet, red, purple, green, in as strong and distinct a pattern as possible will serve as foundation and guide. When the wash is dry, the painter should begin by finding the scale or range or key in which he is to work. This is done by a tentative placing of the most brilliant notes, this time mixed with a medium (white). For instance, one spot will note the color of a white wall in sunlight, another the deep purple-blue shadow in the foliage, a third the glistening green of a corner of the meadow. From these notes there will proceed a gradual building up of the picture, the colors being constantly judged for their inter-

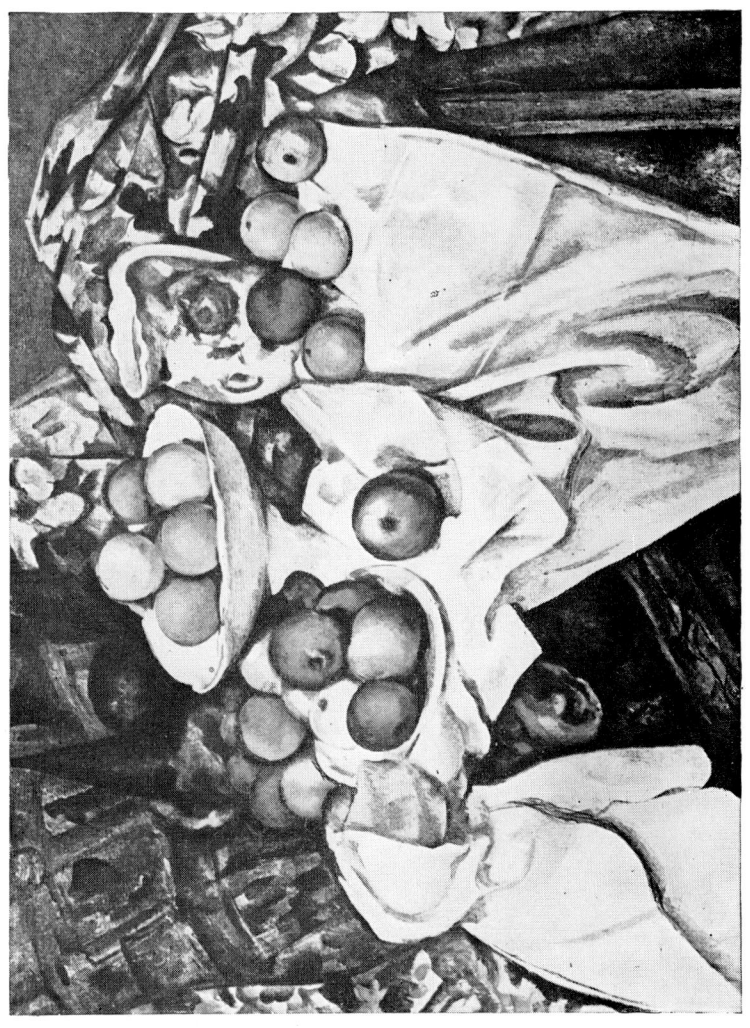

FIGURE 9.—*Still Life* by Cezanne

FIGURE 11.—The simple statement of volume in the mannikin

relations. In this exercise of judgment lies much of the pleasure of painting. Final effect is completely forgotten in the process. The only consideration is to put down color that takes its place without clamoring and without effacing itself. As the study develops, the differentiations in color and quality of color will naturally become more numerous as well as more subtle.

By this method the perplexing problems of color may be attacked by any student with some promise of success. The side of an unpainted barn in shadow may be painted a crude blue. As the sketch progresses, the blue will be modified. Near the ground it will be made to reflect the green of the grass and yet be less green. If too cold, a touch of purple will be brushed over it, or perhaps orange. So the sketch will evolve, a truthful if not a literal statement of the actual scene.

The modification of colors out-of-doors will be accomplished by a slightly different process from that employed in still-life painting. In our indoor studies, where we have wanted to neutralize colors we employed their complementaries, red becoming gray when mixed with green. Out-of-doors, where reflection and refraction give a brilliance and atmospheric character to the scene, we do not want gray to predominate. In place of complementaries we employ "near complementaries." Green will be modified by violet rather than red, and if this combination fails to yield, the violet will in turn be modified by orange. This is a principle of Impressionist or Pointillist painting. It need not, however, be executed in the technique of these schools. A rapid brush stroke of one color over another will permit each color to contribute to the general effect. Any object of an undecided color may be convincingly recorded if we use this means, provided also that we do not sacrifice the dominant note of coolness or warmth. Just as the side of the barn may be painted of blue, green, violet, and orange, so may the shingled roof in sunlight be painted of red-violet and blue-green and yellow-orange and yet appear to the spectator to be nothing more than a yellow-gray. These colors must be used fairly dry, on separate brushes, and brushed into each other cleanly and quickly with as few strokes as possible. Working them together will result in muddy color.

The above method is not a final method, but it has been found to be a very practical one for initiating the student into the mysteries of color out-of-doors. Eventually he will abandon the roundabout system and set down directly the final color. But it is safe to say he will not mix the color of the old mill on his palette until much water has run under it.

We come now to the more prosaic matter of the mechanics of outdoor sketching. The student should work on sketch boards or canvas not smaller than 16″ x 20″. This stricture is laid down to prevent students from developing a "post card" eye which cannot visualize a large composition. A folding easel will be required, and this should be supplied with spikes to grip the ground and with a device for tilting the board or canvas to a vertical position. An easel that does not hold the top of the canvas in a clamp is useless in the wind. The wind will be a great annoyance even to the best easel, but a way of anchoring the tripod in a strong breeze is to suspend a heavy stone from the apex so that it will hang in the center. The easel should be so placed that the rays of the sun will not strike the canvas, for a sketch painted in sunlight will appear distorted and lifeless when brought indoors.

Choice of subject will give some trouble. Confronted with a great expanse of landscape the novice will have difficulty determining how much or how little to include in his picture. The suggestion made earlier, that he confine his first sketches to close-ups, will narrow down the possibilities. Then by means of a cardboard out of which a rectangle, say 3″ x 4″, has been cut, the student will be enabled to delimit his view. Holding the rectangle before the scene and shifting it while looking through it with one eye, he will find one view more interesting and agreeable than another, and so arrive at a definite choice of material. Once having marked the boundaries of the chosen scene upon his canvas he will unconsciously focus his attention upon that fragment of nature.

Now let us repeat the order of attack. With the brush dipped in a thin wash of bluish turpentine a rough and tentative drawing of the scene is made. The procedure is identical with that for still life. The purpose of the drawing is not to arrive at any accurate contour of an object or area but to divide the surface into broad and varied shapes so that no part of it is disproportionately vacant and barren of interest. A picture in which there is a vast stretch of flat sky and a huddled assemblage in a corner beneath it may have literary and dramatic value but will be a poor design from the painter's point of view. In painting, interest comes from variety of shape and size of areas, but not from excessive disparity. The sketches below (Figure 10a and Figure 10b) illustrate an undesirable and a desirable arrangement.

The patterns having been outlined, we proceed to wash in with a clear light turpentine stain (no white in the pigment) the broad divisions of area we have marked. This is the critical test of our choice of subject. If the stain possesses attractive pattern, the possibilities for the success of the sketch are good. If the pattern appears uninteresting, lacking in force and variety of color, we had better wash the canvas clean and try another viewpoint. At no time will the finished study possess better or sharper pattern than in this earliest stage.

FIGURE 10*a*.—An uninteresting arrangement of areas

FIGURE 10*b*.—Areas related in size for interest

From this point the tentative placing of notes which we have described is in order. The lightest, the darkest, the most brilliant are experimentally recorded. If these are related to the satisfaction of the painter, the sketch is then under way. The rest is the gradual relating of color values, as we have seen.

There are, however, some rules and principles worth keeping in mind. Color is best determined by looking through half closed eyes. (The painter's squint is as much a mark of his business as is the sailor's roll.) Then there is the sense of space which should never be lost. Planes of varying color will convey space, that is, recession, much more vividly than smoothly graded color paling toward the horizon. Smooth gradations should in fact be generally avoided. Even the round trunks of trees should be painted in at least three vertical planes to avoid the appearance of being flat strips of cardboard. There are other methods of obtaining the illusion of volume and space. Patterns of warm colors should alternate with patterns of cool color wherever possible. The treatment of foreground should be bold and not overburdened with detail; otherwise, it will stop the eye instead of leading it into the picture. The same principle applies to the sky, the dome effect of which is accomplished by planes of subtly varied color. A clear blue sky may be given concavity by placing passages of cold ultramarine close to the top and working downward with transitional planes of increasing warmth and paleness. Order can be given a study by determining which of several similar colors is the predominant, and subduing the others. For example, if there are several red barns in the landscape, the most intensely red one will be the one best placed to receive attention, the others being restrained, and each if possible given a distinct hue. The same idea of emphasis and diversity applies to clouds. If to these rules and devices is added an attention to the mass and weight and volume of trees, houses, etc., the work resulting should have little in common with the crude daub which is the usual first effort of the art student.

A word as to the length of the sketch period. The beginner will make the most rapid progress by allotting from two to three hours in one session to each sketch. If the sketch is muddy in color or otherwise unsatisfactory, he should make no attempt to improve it or rework it later. He should determine wherein the difficulty lies. If it is the arrangement or pattern that is faulty, he will abandon the subject. But if the fault lies in the quality of the color or the distortion of values or in the lack of order due to too many important points screaming for attention, the best corrective is a fresh sketch. It is more profitable to paint the same scene several times each time anew than to work on one study until it is "completed." Such a completed study is often a corpse of a sketch, something which has been niggled to death. Freshness and vitality are the prime essentials of the sketch. All outdoor work should remain in spirit a sketch, a continued and diligent search for exactitude in color relations, enhanced by certain devices, modified to present an ordered statement.

Sketching out-of-doors should not remain an end in itself. It is a necessary preparation for landscape painting and only a preparation. The material gathered firsthand will be doubly recorded on the brain and on the canvas board to be called upon when the more pretentious landscape composition is undertaken. The elements of such composition are the concern of a later chapter. Before leaving this one, however, a suggestion may be in order: that the student attempt, without any further study of composition beyond the simple arrangement and pattern he already commands, a synthetic picture combining the material of several of his sketches. This of course should be done indoors. Such a first attempt at landscape picture-making will probably not result in a masterpiece but it will be a useful exercise in creative painting. What is perhaps even more important, it will reveal the necessity for the unifying principles of composition.

VIII

POETRY IN THE LANDSCAPE

THE PURSUIT of nature's ever-varying aspects should draw the painting student to the outdoors whenever weather permits. Continued practice will result in a quick command of the palette which temperamental skies exact. All the sport lies in stalking nature's fleeting hues and catching them alive. To bungle and fall behind is to cease being hunter to become only a kind of taxidermist compelled to stuff the scene with shoddy makeshift. Rapid vision, proficiency in application, and control of pigment are requisite to the good sketch artist, but will come of course only after a great deal of practice.

These qualities of the competent painter not only make sketching a pleasure but enable him to lay up authentic material for more pretentious ends, the design and feeling in the landscape picture. The serious student of painting will in the course of time become conscious of esthetic elements in landscape pictures springing from the mind and personality of the artist as much as from the competent report of nature. And so he will come to regard outdoor sketching as an exercise, a phase, a stage in his development, and a gathering of notes for more involved undertakings. He will ask himself what he, as artist, has added to the scene, what he has revealed that is not apparent to the ordinary observer. Comparing his sketches with the paintings of professionals he will feel the absence in his work of superior penetration, of certain laws and truths which underlie the surface appear-

72

ance of things. He will feel the need for rearrangement of the scene the better to clarify and intensify his statement of it. The sketches he has painted are mere reflections at best. He has been giving back to nature no more, perhaps less, than nature has given to him. In short, his exercises were in no real sense art. Art, he remembers, calling to mind a stock of old aphorisms, is personal discovery, superior penetration, imaginative restatement of a theme in such a way as to secure the maximum force of its meaning.

As in still life then, there will arise the question, What is the painter to aim for in the art of landscape? Having passed his preliminary stage and acquired the capacity for recording cleanly and broadly the color effects before him, he must turn his mind's eye away from nature and toward the esthetic mechanism of his canvas. For the art of landscape is very largely the art of composition. This branch of the painter's equipment may be acquired by diligent study. But there is another element, not easy to catalogue or describe, commonly referred to as poetic feeling, which is the margin of difference between the good painting and the really fine one.

The composition itself may be so original and beautifully integrated as to constitute poetry in a plastic sense. Or the style of the painter may endow an ordinary composition with the poetic quality. Recall, for example, the still life of Chardin, its quietude and sensitivity, its detachment from the commonplace. Ordinary utilitarian objects are invested with esthetic quality. The charm imparted is the personal gift of the painter. It is apparent first in the staging, that is, the presentation of the material, or what Berenson calls the "significance" of the scene. The decorative division of space reflects the quality of the painter's mind, his sense of order, of proportion, of harmony. His sensitivity is transfixed into the pigment itself, caressed and scumbled onto the canvas.

These are painting qualities but they are also the result of poetic feeling. Many potboilers are praised for their poetic feeling because writers mistake their sentimental subject matter, their moonlights and hushed twilights, and lovers in a skiff, etc., for poetry expressed plastically. Such painters when sincere are merely soft or are sidetracked in the wrong medium. Real poetic feeling in painting cannot be expressed except in the language of the paint.

The first landscapist to possess poetic gifts similar to Chardin's was Corot (named like the former, Jean Baptiste). Corot discovered poetic quality in the technique of applying pigment to gain the illusion of the softness or downiness of meadow and tree. Landscape obviously lends itself to a much more illusive and mysterious treatment than does the still-life group. The sensitive technique of Chardin became in Corot's hands a Romantic idiom. It also led to much poor imitation and charlatanry. The brush stroke is elusive, mysterious, deceptive. How many uninspired men have passed for poet-painters because they discovered the idiom of the poetic Corot!

It was inevitable that Corot's success in catching the dreamy moods of nature should lead to the establishment of a school of Romantic landscapists whose ideals infiltrated the art of every western country—the Barbizon School. It is not our intention to outline the various schools of landscape art; this one is recalled only because its famous poetic feeling is pertinent to our exposition. The Barbizon painters were painters of moods. To speak of nature's moods is to endow physical aspects of nature with human feelings and this is, of course, Romanticism. Twilight and obscurity, heroic, dying sunsets were easy devices for begging the poetic question. All the moods were captured except those workaday ones of noonday and fair weather. The esthetic achievement (a very de-

batable one) of the Barbizon group was not their trite literature—heroism, death, love, and dreams—but their exploration of the esthetic possibilities in the application of pigment.
No one can resist the real poetry or mystery that lies in the
paint of Monticelli. Unfortunately, the surface of the canvas
was depended upon to convey the poetry. A tradition has
likewise been built around the work of the "great American
mystics," Blakelock and Ryder, because of the way they applied the paint.

While Ryder is generally acknowledged America's great
poet-painter, to some he is an unfulfilled literary poet who
worked, not too expertly, in the wrong medium. He depended upon the indistinct and slurred statement to stir the
imagination. He also depended upon subject matter tradi-
tionally poetic. The landscape painter, if he is to avoid fall-
ing into the easy habit of imitation of poetical effects, must
determine for himself wherein the legitimate poetry in painting lies. He must recognize the difference between a quality
expressed through paint and residing in the paint, and the
extraneous associations evoked by the paint. The real thing
may be found in the most prosaic scenes—in the yard of an
insane asylum, as Van Gogh has shown, or in a street of ware-
houses, as many of our young painters have demonstrated.
When at an exhibition we hear all about us comment on the
painters' poetic feeling, we are most likely listening to those
who like pictures which recall the tender aspects of nature.

Landscape, as we know it today, is a comparatively recent
invention. The experiments and discoveries of Impressionism revolutionized esthetic ideals as well as the technique.
The art of composition made rapid progress after Impressionism, largely as a reaction against the formlessness and lack
of design of the colorists. While the student will find it most
profitable therefore to study contemporary works, he will

miss much if he neglects to look into the history of landscape in relation to periods and peoples, literatures and social ideals. No branch of art so reveals the national taste, the moral values, the psychology of a people. In addition to the insight to be gleaned from such a tour into the past, there is pleasure to be found in the discovery of the sources of much modern and contemporary art. One will seldom find a more modern landscape than El Greco's *View of Toledo,* or finer serenity than in Perugino's backgrounds, better linear rhythm than in Fra Angelico's hilly scenes, or more daring color than in Turner's washes. The majesty of Claude's formal land-scapes lifts the spirit, and Breughel's pictures of the seasons make man feel that the earth was made for his enjoyment.

IX

DRAWING THE FIGURE AND HEAD

THE AMATEUR painter who has served a winter's apprenticeship in still-life painting and experienced the pleasure of
outdoor sketching, should, in his second winter, turn to the
study of the figure and head. Charcoal drawing is essential to
the discovery of worth-while objectives in figure and head
painting. So for several months the paint box will lie closed
while its owner explores good and bad ideas in rendering the
human form.

The customary routine of the art school comprises a year
of drawing from plaster casts (beginning with the ear or nose
or eye and ending with the discus thrower) and a year of copying the nude in charcoal, supplemented with studies of the
head, as preparation for painting. All this I have found to be
unnecessary and not productive of good painters. Beyond
developing the eye for accuracy it does not teach the student
how to see. In fact, it is detrimental to his development as a
painter because (1) it substitutes consideration of smart
charcoal handling as an end in itself, (2) it focuses the attention unduly upon anatomy of which he will have very little
need unless he plans to become a medical illustrator, (3) it
prevents him, because of the first two concerns, from seeing
the simple volumes of the figure and the plane surfaces of
head and figure which express these volumes, (4) it avoids the
most important objective in all drawing as art—the design
of line.

77

Much more rapid progress can be made through one little prop, the wooden mannikin. This can be obtained in several sizes; the ten-inch one is adequate. Those I have seen and used were made in Italy, priced at about four dollars. The joints are hinged with wooden pins or are fitted into sockets affording considerable freedom of movement. Since there is no muscular articulation, the student is not distracted by complicated surface contours and may concentrate his attention upon the simple volumes such as the spheroid head, cylindrical arms and legs, etc. The academic way of drawing is to record, with the accuracy of a seismograph record, the bulges, dips, and intervening variations of the contour, stopping occasionally to explain joints and ligatures. The drawing is then skillfully shaded to resemble a photograph. In bygone days almost every student underwent this form of discipline until he had won at least one honorable mention. Alas, how few recipients of the honor have escaped the baneful effects of such apprenticeship sufficiently to paint an acceptable figure! The mannikin invites a very different kind of seeing more nearly related to the art of painting.

Begin first with soft charcoal (Imported Vine, price per box 40¢, is best) on newsprint paper (pad 18" x 22" is 25¢). Break off a one-inch piece of charcoal and with the flat side quickly suggest the volumes as they appear to be built up. Note the planes of torso and hips. Use point of charcoal to define simple contour. Put the mannikin in any position, on its back, on its ear, standing, off balance, etc. Constant practice will correct shortcomings in relating proportions. See the illustration (Figure 11).

This drawing from the mannikin has in its favor the development of a correct point of view with regard to the human figure. The impatience of the amateur to draw the nude without any specific preparation or objective generally results in a faulty copy of meandering contours, as lacking in geometrical volumes as a sack of sawdust. No training is even worse than too much plaster-cast drawing. But with the training in seeing which the mannikin affords, the student should be able to resolve the living model into the forms which the wooden shapes taught him were basic.

Further, the essential objectives in drawing from the model (always considered as preparation for the painting) are the articulation of the movement of the body and the selectivity of line for purposes of design. The body is capable of much twisting, turning, bending, tension, relaxation; the mannikin is not. The student should pursue this action without losing sight of the volumes. (The matter of design of line is discussed in a special chapter. But since the other two objectives, volume and movement, are enough to keep the amateur draughtsman busy for a season, there should be no hurry to acquire the third.)

A few suggestions may be of help to the beginner in the life class. A common fault is to make the drawing too small. Use standard charcoal sheets 19" x 25" and make the figure (if standing) extend to within a half inch of top and bottom. This will facilitate correct proportion; for if the center of the figure (generally the crotch) is made to coincide with the center of the paper, there will be little likelihood of making serious errors.

To find the center of the figure we hold a thin stick or brush at arm's length (the arm must be rigid) and looking at it against the model we mark a point from head to crotch, and compare this distance with that from crotch to foot until the exact center is found. The thumb sliding up and down the stick serves as marker.

Common faults in proportion are making the head too large or too small and hands and feet too small. To overcome the first relate the length of head to the chest by measurement. Relate hands and feet to forearm and lower part of leg respectively.

Having noted the general proportions, attempt by means of a single line from chin to ankle to indicate the action of the figure. Then note relation of the angle of the hips to the angle of the shoulders. If the weight of the figure rests on one foot, these lines will most likely oppose each other in their diagonal direction.

Note: The movement of the figure will not be convincing unless the foot which carries the weight is correctly placed in vertical relation to the head. For the inexperienced draughtsman a plumb line will be indispensable for finding this relation.

With these few directions established, build up the volumes of the figure as if you were working, like the sculptor, with a solid material. The important thing will be to make one volume grow out of the other without awkwardness or distortion. Often a beginner's drawing will have the head improperly placed on the shoulders. There is a way to prevent this error. Find the small hollow between the two collar bones and from this point draw two diagonal lines to points on the head where the earlobes begin. If the head is so turned that only one ear is visible draw to the point you know the earlobe to be. Then drop two perpendicular lines to the chest and build up shoulders with triangles. Figure 12a and b will illustrate this device.

The head and neck so placed will be well constructed, but the contour seen will of course vary somewhat according to individual characteristics. All the forms of the body should be resolved into the most simple geometrical patterns—the ovoids of the large shoulder muscles, for example, the oval of the abdomen, the triangles of the shoulder blades. It is better for the student to work out his own system of geometry than to accept a ready-made one. This is my objection to such handbooks on figure drawing as Bridgman's *Figure Construction*. In that classic the author presents the student with a pat system for recording the figure and the result is that the student does not see the model, but concentrates his attention upon copying the clever technique of the author. As preparation for painting, such drawing is valueless. There is more solid substance in Vanderpoel's *The Human Figure*, but unfortunately the author's drawings contradict the intellectual character of his approach. These drawings are nicely

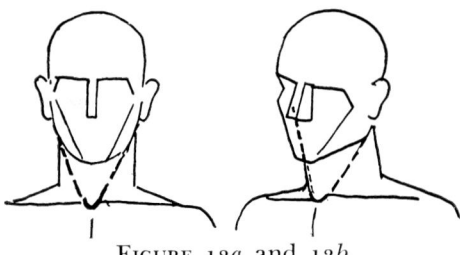

FIGURE 12*a* and 12*b*

done and pretty but have little in them beyond the photographic ideal.

Thousands of students have imitated the Vanderpoel style. It is surprising how many finished drawings one may see in the life class which show great diligence in the handling of detail yet lack the feeling of tension, relaxation, movement of the body. Yet these qualities should be caught in the first half hour of the pose. Practice in expression of movement is much more beneficial to the student than nice craftsmanship or diagrammatic illustration of what goes on anatomically under the skin.

It may be objected by academicians that the lack of emphasis upon anatomical study will handicap the student who hopes to paint from the nude. To this objection there is a most concrete answer—the *Odalisque* of Ingres, which hangs in the Louvre. Ingres is acknowledged by all factions of artists to have been one of the great draughtsmen of history. Volumes of his drawings are source books for teachers of life drawing and anatomy. Yet his *Odalisque,* a beautiful nude, has three vertebrae too many and her breast which is seen from under her arm appears to be attached to her armpit. There are other impossible statements in the drawing of this figure. Yet the painting is accepted as a masterpiece, which it undoubtedly is by reason of its linear design and its stylization. The tacit indorsement of this picture as a major work of art should be proof enough that accurate anatomy is no guarantee of excellence in painting the nude, and conversely, that its absence does not prevent the excellent painting.

The painting of the head requires as much study as that of the entire figure. The plane structure of the head with its protruding features is a complex problem even when seen at eye level from the front. Capable of much turning and tilting, it presents so many problems in foreshortening and perspective that the amateur is likely to resort to drawing faces rather than heads. Yet it is possible by means of diagrams called construction lines to record and explain the head's many movements. Here I shall introduce a collection of such diagrams which I believe are self-explanatory. (Figure 13)

The use of the living model for practice in head drawing is obligatory (because of foreshortening or perspective). The student is cautioned not to be sidetracked by the complex modeling of puffs, bumps, wrinkles, etc. of the individual but to proceed in a logical, systematic manner, first putting down the oval of the face (about 8″) and then building up the construction lines. By this method he will not become

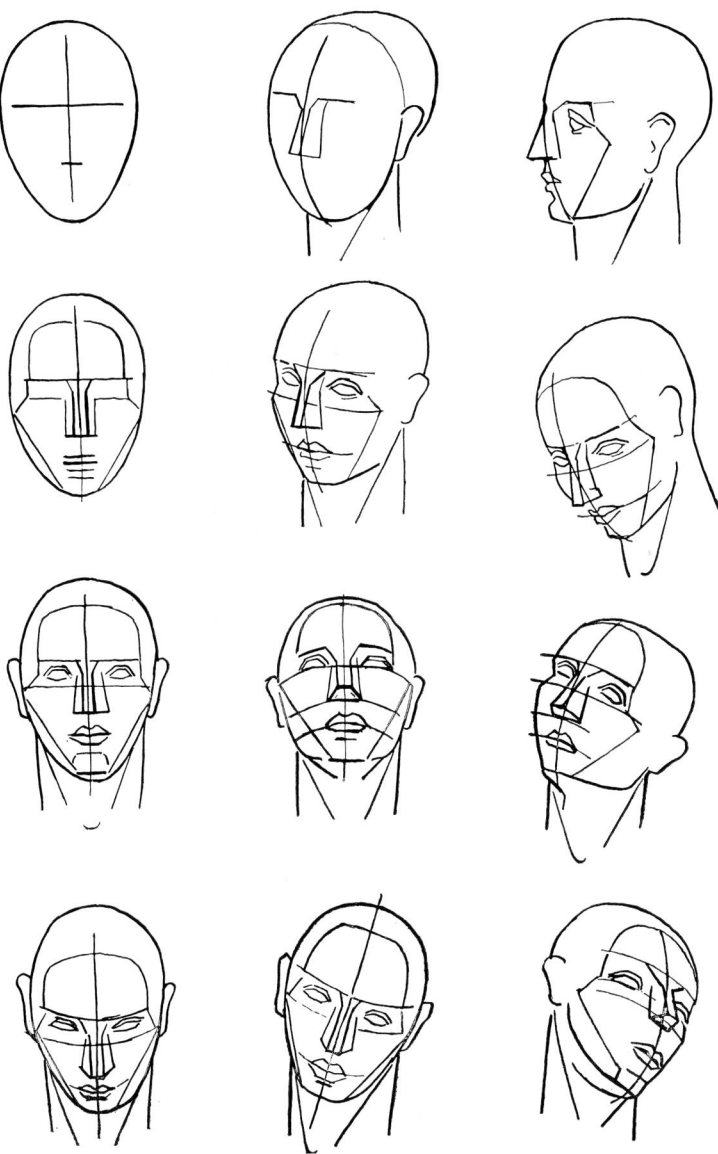

FIGURE 13.—Construction of the head

confused in placing planes and features. This done he should use the flat side of the charcoal to express the volumes and surfaces of the head and, as in the case of the mannikin drawings, give a more precise delineation to the entire mass with the point of the charcoal. Figure 14 shows this procedure.

X

PAINTING THE FIGURE AND HEAD

WHEN THE painter has worked zealously as draughtsman for several months, he should return to that helpful little prop, the mannikin, for a short interval of study preliminary to painting the nude. The mannikin may be painted several times against simple pieces of drapery of decided color. There will result from this experience some facility in finding the color of planes of light and dark in their relation to the background. If the planes are made of various values of one color, or one batch of pigment, the painting will be nothing more than a tinted drawing; but if each plane is carefully observed for its variations in hue, the first step toward the painting of the human form will have been made.

It is true that the color and texture of skin present difficulties in nude painting for which practice with the mannikin is no preparation. However, this is not the all important matter today that it was twenty years ago. The fine nudes of Carl Hofer, the German, or of Eberl, Segonzac, Favory, and other contemporary French painters, show little concern for the iridescent color and silky texture of skin. It rests with the individual how far he wants to pursue this surface imitation; practice from the living model will reward him with the formula.

The really desirable objectives in painting the human figure are encompassed in the one word design. The lines and accents of the body should be arranged in a rhythmical order. The volumes of head, chest, hips, legs, and arms may be designed with regard to the scheme of light. But this is looking far ahead and is mentioned here only to show the relative unimportance of texture.

In posing the model arrange the areas of the background in such a way that parts of the figure are seen against patterns of different color or value. Stain the figure in one flat wash (also all the other parts of the canvas) before attempting to paint the various volumes. Relate the large values of the parts of the figure, then suggest the planes. Do not attempt to paint the head except as an ovoid mass. See that the planes are not just light and dark, but warm or cool as the form demands.

After two or three studies of the nude have been made, it will be a good plan to attempt the painting of the head. Experience in this branch of the art is fundamental to good nude painting. Furthermore, no amateur should neglect a field which can reward the painter so richly by its combinations of interesting plastic qualities and friendly associations. It is suggested, therefore, that the student spend some little while in the study of head painting before returning to the nude.

Painting a head and portrait painting as we know it today are not precisely the same thing. A portrait is a painting done to order, and it is natural that certain mannerisms and compromises should result from the demands of client or patron and of social convention. It seems the portrait must have elegance and starch at the expense of honest painting. It has not always been so. In the art of the past there are many notable examples of portraits that are marvels of straightforward statement. In the Louvre is a painting of an old man

PAINTING THE FIGURE AND HEAD

and his grandson by Ghirlandaio, in which the old man's diseased and bulbous nose is recorded with as much minute care as are the charming features of the boy. One may well speculate on the treatment of this subject by society portraitists. The repulsive feature would very likely be reduced to a fraction above normal and its texture lost in a maze of clever technique. In the Prado in Madrid is (or was before the Spanish Civil War) the famous Velasquez Room. Much of the impressiveness of this collection may be attributed to the Spanish master's paintings of dwarfs. The models who posed for these portraits would, if we met them, repel us by their monstrous proportions; but seeing them on the canvas we are fascinated by the exactness of description and the skill of statement. In truth, the heads of these dwarfs are more forthrightly painted than most of the royal portraits acclaimed by critics. Some of the latter pictures are patently done to formula, extremely skillful but nevertheless revealing the influence of the fashionable Rubens. They seem to say to the student, this is how the chin of royalty should be painted, and this is the proper color for a young princess' nose. There is, no doubt, much pleasure to be had in demonstrating a formula while painting a royal personage. But if Velasquez' nature was not greatly unlike that of the good artists of today, he found much more satisfaction in recording the forms and traits of models who were in no position to demand a flattering report of their features.

The cleavage between honest head painting and clever portraiture reaches its widest with the beginnings of modern art, or Postimpressionism. But it dates a generation earlier to the work of Courbet. His art began as a protest against the kind of sleight of hand to which the followers of Manet were addicted. Manet himself had made a virtue of his remarkable facility. He painted both honestly and cleverly.

He caught the grace of feature as well as its idiosyncrasy. But his easy sweeping stroke gave ideas to students unendowed with his capacity and intellectual honesty—principally the idea of dazzling the layman with a tricky bravura. Courbet boldly defied this trend and its apologists but was unable to stem the tide of fashion. The brush stroke became the measure of art. The painter Carolus-Duran, acclaimed by society, established a school of smart technique. A host of painters, many Americans among them, flocked to study with this most adept virtuoso. When at the end of the century social portraiture in its natural course reached a kind of conventional craft empty of all vitality, its death as an art was marked by the appearance of the work of three sincere, conscientious, and vital artists—Van Gogh, Renoir, and Cezanne.

Van Gogh focused attention upon ordinary working class types and the surprising beauty in homely faces honestly painted. Renoir, apparently regarding smart brush work as a personal intrusion, showed the possibilities of expressing the volume and color of a head. He was a more subtle exponent of honest portraiture. The brush in his hand was loaded with charm as well as with paint. But this charm had nothing to do with falsification in the interest of romantic elegance. If he did not stress the imperfections of feature as did Van Gogh, it was because he subdued features to the sense of volume and roundness of the head. This was accomplished by delicate modeling, with color of the transparency of china. Critics repelled by Van Gogh's bluntness of statement were forced to accept Renoir's classical precepts because they were phrased so enchantingly. He might be a rebel, but there was no denying he possessed good taste. This made him respectable. Perhaps this is why his theories were so readily adopted by a whole school of prominent American painters and teachers such as K. H. Miller, Speicher, Glackens, etc. Unfortunately, the Renoir technique is often stressed at the expense of the major ideal, the principle of living volume.

Our principal interest, however, lies in the painting of Cezanne. His heads, first ridiculed and rejected by the knowing, have come to be patterns of study for all but the social portraitists and most conservative classes in art schools. His methods of construction are as logical as geometry, his color as functional as it is rich. (When we speak of functional color we mean the use of color not for its appealing decorative value, as in the work of Gauguin, but in order to reveal or intensify the form of the object. For instance, if we show three sides of a cube in isometric view and paint each side a different color, we add to the clarity of the statement that the cube presents three distinct planes in this particular position. A further explanation is to be found in the chapter on the spatial relation.) Cezanne made color express the many planes of the head. His work is at once less seductive and pretty than Renoir's and less brutal and emotionally insistent than Van Gogh's. Its value for us lies not so much in the ultimate esthetic ideals which it embodies (which the painter himself could not put into words) as in its rôle of laboratory demonstration of head construction in color. This method of construction will be our aim.

The head of our first model should be one in which the plane surfaces are sharply marked. By this we do not mean that the skin should be lined or wrinkled, or even that the head should necessarily be gaunt and bony. We say of some faces that they are indefinite or shapeless, of others that they appear to be chiseled of marble. It is the latter type, whether young or old, male or female, which we prefer for its definite planes.

In posing the model we had better place him on a box or

platform. We work in a standing position, and if the model is seated, we will be looking down on the top of his head unless we raise him to eye level. Having him face the light will afford the group the best opportunity to trace the design of light from almost any position. The model should stare straight in front of him only long enough to permit his focal point to be noted in order that his pose may be taken correctly after rest periods. At all other times he should be permitted to gaze where he will as otherwise the strain will exhaust him. Twenty-minute poses and three-minute rests will be most satisfactory to both model and painter, although it is customary to pose professionals twenty-five minutes with a five-minute rest.

The head is placed on the canvas with the brush, the oval being made slightly larger than the span of the hand, about eight and a half inches. The usual turpentine stain follows. The patterns made by hair, background, and clothes are washed in until no white spot or area remains. The oval of the head is stained a pink orange. As in still life and landscape, no medium is used with the pigment, only the turpentine. (The covering up of bare spots on the canvas will permit the correct relationship of color.) The staining completed we proceed to construct the head in drawing, using the brush with a light blue pigment to mark off the largest planes. The eyes are not drawn at all, as the sockets must be painted before they can be placed. When these simple areas are made, the business of applying pigment begins.

A parenthetical warning to the student prone to short cuts or perfect systems: There are still some painters who make a finished drawing in charcoal on the canvas, shading it carefully and omitting no detail which will emphasize the likeness to the sitter. They fix the drawing with a spray of shellac and alcohol, and all that remains is to tint a square inch at a time until the canvas is covered. This is pure craft and formula and could not possibly result in true painting because the color is necessarily arbitrary, there being no basis for relationship. Planes of related color are as necessary to the painting of a head as the steel structure is to a skyscraper. To begin at the top of the canvas and work down is as illogical as building a ship by rigging up a topsail before there is a hull. The impatient student must put the matter of likeness out of his mind. It will come of itself if the construction is correct. Likeness is more a matter of correct form than of contour of feature.

The palette should be carefully prepared before the actual painting begins. At top center is the mass of zinc white, and this should be worked into each of the colors on the left side of the palette. The nuances of flesh will prove difficult to the beginner and for this reason the color is combined with the white where it may be picked up in weak hues. Several batches of pigment most demanded should be mixed in advance. Zinc yellow, vermilion, and white should form one; orange, alizarin, and white a second; orange, cobalt, and white a third. On the right side of the palette a batch of orange, green, and white should be worked out from the viridian, and below the ultramarine a violet-blue ranging to red-violet should be mixed. Flesh color in bright light may be made of various combinations of the yellows and reds, but when a cold bluish passage occurs, a whitened cobalt may be brushed over the yellowish white first applied. The half-lights and shadows will present the greatest difficulties. Here the orange-green and the purple-violet combinations may be played against each other until the warm or cool note seen dominates. This combination gives a much more transparent effect of shadow than the browns of sienna and bitumen once exclusively used.

The beginner will find that his studies are apt to be cold in color or chalky. Just as the landscape sketch requires a higher key than the indoor still life, so the head requires a much lower key than would at first appear. The high key is generally chosen because of the texture of the skin which reflects the light and leads the novice to use an almost pure white to indicate the skin's refraction. He has only to hold the color on his brush against the model to see how much darker the lightest note actually is.

Having selected his color range the painter proceeds to give form to the head by means of the intervening values and the warmth and coolness of color. The forehead is painted in at least three vertical planes. The front and side planes of the cheek will appear warmer in color than the forehead. The bridge of the nose will catch the light, while the planes to the sides will be comparatively grayish. The chin will be painted in at least four planes. The eye sockets are given the correct value between half-light and shadow. The whole oval form is indicated by the graying planes as the sides recede from the front of the face. And just as the illusion of roundness is obtained from side to side, so it is gained by making both the forehead and lower part of the face appear to recede. Plate IV shows this stage of the painting. It will be noted that the mouth and eyes do not yet appear. Only when the entire head is well divided into functional planes of color are these features added. They should then be painted in at least three planes to express their form and roundness.

Now it is not to be assumed that a head can be painted by the novice in such one, two, three order. Color in still life will be found difficult enough, but in the transparent skin

PLATE IV.—Building the head in planes of color

reflecting cold lights and having a texture of its own, the painting of subtle passages will tax the skill of the most expert. Fine quality of color in the head is rarely attained even by professionals; therefore, the amateur should feel no discouragement at floundering and unwittingly graying his color. For him the important thing is not quality of color but correct color value. Each area must be as light and as dark as necessary to make it take its place in the general design of roundness. This is not a matter of inspired brushwork, of consummate technique, but only a process of seeing and thinking. At least there is a definite architecture one may follow.

The illustration in color does not pretend to represent a stage in the development of a head as painted by a professional painter. The trained artist does not need to build the structure up in this manner and then obliterate the scaffolding. Planes and structure are so well understood that the process occurs in the mind of the artist unconsciously, determining the stroke of the brush without impeding its spontaneity. But the beginner will go farther and faster by making such painted charts rather than by turning out clever and dexterous impressions.

However, lest he feel that rigidly constructed studies prevent the expression of his own spontaneous reactions to the model, he may vary his exercises with the sport of an occasional piece of interpretative painting. After two or three sessions have been devoted to painting the structure of a head as outlined, he may then, putting his serious study aside, attempt in one sitting to restate his digested material in more flexible form (see Plate V). It is only after a winter's experience in such a schedule that he may take the liberty of dispensing with the structural chart and give over five or six sessions to working directly from the model, each passage being recorded as observed. By that time the habit of seeing the face in planes will have become established and form will be automatically incorporated into the free and direct expression.

PLATE V.—Emphasizing the abstract or design elements of a head

XI

EXPANDING THE PALETTE

THE PALETTE (selection of pigments) recommended is excellently suited for making quick emphatic statements of color as in the study or sketch. For outdoor painting where light and brilliance are of the essence, no better choice is possible. Moreover it has the virtue of being logical since it is based not upon a particular usage but upon the hues of the prism. Nevertheless, there are certain limitations inherent in the pigments; the very purity and brilliance of them may lead to overstatement, and the intensity of them to a color scheme which tires the eye.

Brilliant color is not necessarily effective color. Too often it is effective only for a very short time, which is to say not effective at all. A poster designed to stop you while you are rushing to an important engagement will use brilliant complementaries. A painting designed to grow into your consciousness and never tire you will be composed of odd harmonies (or dissonances) in which the *quality* of the color will be quite as important as the color itself. This quality is the degree of luminosity of the pigment, its intensity or dullness, reflection or absorption. Since our prismatic colors are generally brilliant and intense, the balance necessary to effective color statement will be too difficult to obtain without the aid of more opaque, less luminous pigments, the earth colors. Further, the treatment of volume and space through color is based upon just these qualities, luminosity and opacity, as

95

will be demonstrated later in the chapter on space composition.

It is possible by means of our prismatic pigments and black to approximate the earth colors through much mixing. But there seems little point to spending a great deal of time putting together expensive pigments such as the cadmiums in order to obtain the equivalent of the most inexpensive ones. Aside from the poor economy, the element of time is more important than it would appear, as vitality in a study is generally the result of direct and sure statement made possible by having the color at hand.

To make clear the advantages of earth colors let us paint a hypothetical picture. In front of an olive green screen we place a model stand painted a warm gray. On the stand we put a small mahogany table with a bowl of oranges upon it. Beside the table is placed a sand-colored Windsor chair. This is the setting for our model, and it being Sunday, we are able to secure a ruddy-faced laborer much dressed in his clean straw hat and black suit. We seat him in the chair and ask him to relax. He removes his hat exposing a thatch of iron-gray hair. He rests a sunburnt hand on the edge of the table. He crosses his knees and places the straw hat over a knee as upon a hatrack. This is the picture. It will be observed that the key is low and that warm color predominates.

With great speed we approximate the color pattern of the picture, using our pure pigments as a turpentine stain. The oranges are red-orange and so are the hands and face. The table is purple in certain areas and so is the black suit. The gray hair and the gray model's stand are both scrubbed in with cobalt and orange. The sand-colored chair is suggested in the same pigments, the orange predominating. This rough statement of color values will do as a point of departure, but it is certainly not exact. We depend upon the zinc white to mitigate the intensity of the stain, to give body and depth to the color.

The turpentine wash having dried, we begin to approximate the actual colors. The background must be determined first, as it establishes a basis for all relationship. The orange-green stain is much too intense. We add white to the two colors but it does not sufficiently diminish the brilliance of the mixture. We resort to complementaries and add a bit of vermilion or alizarin. We must add a touch of blue and a touch of yellow and even then the quality of the color is unsatisfactory. How much better it would be to use terre-verte (earth green) straight out of the tube. Also how much less expensive if the cadmium and viridian are of good makes. We may pile on this color without that painful reluctance so often observed in art students.

The same necessity for exactitude of hue and quality dictate the use of other earth colors in our figure painting. Comparing the brown-red hand and face of the sitter with the bright note of orange made by the fruit in the bowl we see that our stain is incorrect. The rich complexion requires less luminosity; it has something of the heavy quality of the color of brick. The pigment on our palette can be made to match the color, but the probability is that its quality will be too intense or too chalky; or if mixed with too many graying factors, too murky. A touch of Venetian or Indian red in our ordinary flesh mixture would give the precise hue and density to the color. Indian red is a richer and deeper (more purple) pigment than the Venetian, although some companies make them identical and interchangeable.[1] Both are made from chemical waste but behave exactly as the earth colors and are fairly permanent.

[1] For the chemical content of these and other colors referred to in this chapter see Doerner's *The Materials of the Artist.*

Another use for the Indian red will be found when we come to match the color of the mahogany table. The orange-purple combination used in the stain results in a stained-glass effect. The cool blue sheen over the red-brown can of course be suggested by the Impressionist method of broken color. But as we do not wish to be restricted to usages of a bygone day, we had better discover other pigments capable of conveying the color and texture with a minimum of mixing and brushwork. A violet made of alizarin and ultramarine and white added to the Indian red will make the color we want.

Our model's Sunday coat of black presents another problem for our limited palette. The obvious pigment for painting black is black. Why then should this color be banned from the beginner's list? The answer is that the inexperienced student will get it into all his clean pigment with disastrous results. And what is equally as important, its presence on the palette will retard his experience in the mixing of pure colors for neutral effects. So black is at first banned. We assume now that the student has reached this chapter by the route marked out and so has had the requisite experience. As a reward we present him with ivory black.

Black is a "color" which cannot well be omitted from the indoor palette. Out-of-doors a black garment undergoes many mutations in half-light, sun, and shadow. One side may appear a brown-orange, the other a cold deep blue. But indoors the rusty or steely hues can be convincingly painted only as overtones—that is, when the area has already been covered with black pigment. The black most in use is ivory black. It is seldom used pure as it is apt to be outside the tonal range of value; also it is too transparent. (Pure white is likewise avoided.) Another reason why painters seldom employ the black pure is that they are very much concerned with catching the many colorful nuances which lights and reflections impart.

In lighter mixtures black will give a certain restraint to color which a prismatic palette lacks in indoor work. Our hypothetical figure, for instance, has iron-gray hair. This we tentatively represent with a gray wash made of cobalt and orange. With the white added the combination is neutral enough but has a secondary quality of transparence in place of the flat metallic hue. So while it is well suited for the warm gray of the model's stand, it fails to give the silvery quality which simple black and white can impart. The experienced painter will mix his gray flat and vary it with overtones of pure color just as he does with black and with white.

Two other colors in our figure painting will require new pigments if we wish to avoid excessive mixing and at the same time reach a more exact quality. Both of these colors are yellows. The pale but dense yellow of the new straw hat may be adequately rendered by Naples yellow just as it comes from the tube. This fat, well-spreading pigment is the color of a sandy dirt road in the morning sunlight. It is permanent except when brought into contact with the palette knife or when mixed with cadmiums. These exceptions impose considerable restriction upon the painter and have therefore made the pigment unpopular. The other yellow is a yellow-brown, also of great density. It is the familiar yellow ochre, the standby of house painter and artist alike. Our clay-yellow Windsor chair will be painted with this color raised in value by a touch of white. This earth pigment has no luminosity or transparency and so makes a desirable contrast to the purer yellows we have so far used. It is not suited to delicate textures or subtle play of lights upon the skin but is indispen-

sable for opaque surfaces. Mixed with the prismatic colors
its heaviness (opacity) dominates the combination even when
its color does not.

Thus we see our figure study completed with the aid of
earth colors new to our palette. The intensity and high key
which mark the prismatic palette are gone. However, the student should not therefore immediately abandon the list of
colors with which he began. This list may remain fixed for a
long time. New pigments should be introduced gradually
and these are best arranged on the right vertical side of the
palette. It is to be hoped that eventually he will know enough
of the special qualities of paints to set his palette with the
least number of colors, and these specially selected for each
particular composition.

In addition to the pigments just used two other earth colors
will be found invaluable to the exploring student. These are
burnt sienna and raw umber. There are also a raw sienna
and a burnt umber, but they are not very desirable for the
following reasons. Raw sienna absorbs a great amount of oil
in its manufacture and consequently tends to darken quickly.
It is a very transparent brown of a yellowish hue, used a great
deal by the old masters in the glazing process (repeated
washes of color in varnish) but not so well suited to our
present-day technique. (A pigment similar in hue, somewhat
lighter in value is the very permanent and beautiful gold
ochre.) Burnt umber has the same defect of rapid darkening.
In addition it is apt to "bleed," that is, to come through to
the surface in little spots and blisters. The first two colors
are more permanent, and in addition possess certain qualities
which make them a boon to the subtle colorist. The heavy
greenish-brown hue of raw umber can be used by the sensitive composer to give a weight and balance to an otherwise

too luminous or intense color arrangement. It is opaque and buttery, without luminosity or incandescence. The burnt sienna on the other hand is an intensely hot transparent brown. Also widely used in centuries past for glazing, it is still a requisite of the paint box since it is especially adapted (in conjunction with prismatic colors, except possibly alizarin) for the painting of luminous shadows and shadowy passages in skin or flesh. In such passages a heavy blackness would destroy the textural quality of skin, its reflective surface; the burnt sienna keeps the darks transparent.

Let us turn from browns and the more neutral pigments to some other so-called "pure" colors. Certain blues and reds whose acquaintance we have not yet made will add flexibility and exactness to our palette. For landscape or outdoor sketching a most useful pigment is cerulean blue. Pure and intense in color, it is closely related to cobalt, although much heavier in body. As its name indicates, it is particularly adapted to the painting of skies whose slightly greenish cast eludes other blues. However, it must be used judiciously, that is, sparingly, as otherwise it will give the picture a cloying quality. It is for this reason often disdained by painters as a "Christmas candy" color.

Another blue that can be controlled only by experts is Prussian blue. While this color is permanent enough, it is of such strength as to destroy the effectiveness of other colors in the composition unless carefully managed. It is a deep greenish-blue, in value about the same as ultramarine. (Cerulean is much lighter.) While it is strong in its action, it is not as pure as the other blues and for this reason is both desirable and undesirable—undesirable as a substitute for either ultramarine or cerulean because it grays the mixtures, desirable in odd harmonies, particularly with yellow-browns and dull greens. It is recommended with hesitancy as its assertive nature can make havoc with the composition of an inexpert colorist.

While our battery of reds (with its latest addition, Indian red) is well prepared to take care of the hues we are likely to encounter in landscape and still life, it will prove inadequate in the painting of portrait or head. The variety of coloring and texture of skin will surprise and often disconcert the inexperienced painter. He may take a leaf from the notebook of the cosmetic industry which has long recognized the many nuances in the female complexion. The many hues and shades of rouge on the market are proof that a blush is not such a simple affair. About the year 1925, painters in Paris derived considerable pleasure (it appeared) from doing the highly rouged faces of hard women with indiscriminate gobs of vermilion. But that only went to show how ineptly the subject handled her own beauty problem. The portrait artist will try every sort of bright red as long as it is of good make, and will come to rely upon those he can best handle. A few are here recommended to the student. Our cadmium red is made in at least two hues, the light and ordinary. English vermilion is close to the light hue, perhaps a trifle more scarlet. Harrison red and prismatic red are supposedly pure red. There are also many light and dark shades of vermilion, of varying density and transparency, according to make. The cadmium has the advantage over the vermilions in that it is not only permanent, that is, free from the effects of atmospheric change, but is also more compatible with other pigments, particularly those on our palette.

A cooler darker red closely related to the alizarin is rose madder. It is slightly more violet and more delicate than the alizarin and has even less body. It has been used by the old masters for glazing, but today is used principally by portrait-

ists to make the subtle tints of flesh and the delicate coloring
of lips. The natural product is a dye taken from the madder
plant. While no color can take its place in giving the transparent tinge of rose that marks certain complexions, its per-
manency is doubtful. It often fades and sometimes bleeds.
There are, however, synthetic rose madders (such as sun-
proof rose) made from coal-tar and quite dependable, and our
very reliable ultramarine red. The painter should make an
effort to learn in which makes these may be obtained.

These colors (to recapitulate, Indian red, green earth,
ivory black, Naples yellow, yellow ochre, burnt sienna, raw
umber, and synthetic rose madder) should be enough for the
advanced student to experiment with. Combined with the
prismatic colors the variations are almost limitless, especially
when used with black and white.

Black is the most productive and magical of all agents,
changing the character of colors when used sparingly and
with imagination. Odd greens may be made with yellows and
black, odd blues with white, ultramarine and black, odd pur-
ples with alizarin and black, and odd violets with alizarin,
ultramarine, and black. Black not only mixes into unusual
hues but used in heavy outline or rhythm will set off a particular color in its greatest brilliance and intensity. Used
pure in small patterns it will enrich the composition particularly when one primary or prismatic color dominates the picture. The inventive use of black as a color rather than as a
dark value is of comparatively recent origin dating to the
early 1900's. Even so, its use is for the most part a practice
of Modernism (see the work of Rouault, Gromaire, Vlaminck, Picasso), our academic painters showing no interest in
such new departures. The Impressionist palette was good
enough for father.

Previous to Impressionism black was used quite as extensively as today, perhaps more so. But it was used generally in combination with browns to produce impenetrable shadows, deep accents, and strong modeling. In other words, the painting was often regarded as a tinted drawing shaded in black. The effect of chiaroscuro thus obtained had for its models the work of Rembrandt and Leonardo and perhaps the more theatrical art of the Spanish painter Ribera. The use of black as pattern in flat design was introduced into European art in the latter half of the nineteenth century. Manet and Whistler both sought in the Japanese print authority and example for this innovation. Black became not a color, however, but a decorative area, like the silhouette. When Pissarro and others launched the scientific investigation of color through the study of the prism and the structure of the eye, black ceased to be, for a time at least, an important element in the painter's materials.

The Impressionists dispelled the sombreness and gloom of the Dutch interior. They abolished all the earth colors declaring there was nothing in nature not demonstrably composed of atoms of prismatic color. So black was ruled to be nonexistent. This decree, while relieving the world, or at any rate the art gallery, of darkness, produced another kind of esthetic calamity—a universe all rosy and baby blue. But not all painters, even at the height of this movement, were won over to its canons. For example, the famous Munich School (which trained two of our most interesting painters, Chase and Duveneck) ignored the color systems and theories of the Pissarro-Monet order of broken, prismatic color. Its method was an impressionism achieved by smart brush work in chiaroscuro, light forms emerging in impasto from thick bitumen and black. With the virtuosos of the Sargent type, black was used primarily for rapid, dashing accents, to set off in sharp relief, and with little intervening modeling, the light forms of the figure. Black became a real color only when the modern movement got under way with the experiments of the Parisian group self-styled Les Fauves.

The many diversified and often contradictory programs of Modernism have at least one common motive of rebellion— a protest against the degradation of the art to a performer's craft. The one intention was to restore painting to its former status as a composer's art, not a player's. To make rare harmonies of color and to organize these within a preconceived form was the unavowed purpose of many isms. True, the color harmonies differed and the forms differed with each fresh esthetic program launched by a new clique. But the experimentation with color was tremendously stimulated. Painting was released from its servitude to drawing and to story and became, like music, an art resting on its compositional qualities to affect the emotions and awaken the plastic imagination.

To Modernism, then, we owe many new usages of color. Not the least of these is the use of black. The Cubists have produced many inventive canvases in which black and various values of black-gray have been combined with ochrous colors to form subdued and distinguished harmonies. Abstractionists like Kandinsky have made compositions in which several blacks of different texture and quality were played against each other. One black might be matt, another transparent, a third thick and oily. One might have a bluish cast, another a rusty overtone. One might appear to be a plane distant in space, another a plane close to the surface. White, hitherto regarded only as a medium for other pigment, is just as imaginatively employed. In all Kandinsky's work the many qualities of a color have been explored to the utmost, so that one passage will often appear to be unrelated to another passage of the same color when the degree of intensity or transparency

is altered. It is often asserted that this modernist's designs
are fragmentary, effeminate, dehumanized, morbid, etc. But
if his place as a composer of exquisite harmonies is debatable,
his contributions to the expressiveness of color are worthy of
the admiration of the most conservative and academic artists.
(Psychologists too may find it profitable to study from his
work the sensory effect of *quality* of color as they have in the
past studied reactions to colors.)

The last two decades have brought to light many other
gifted composers working in odd harmonies. As we are not
concerned with compendious records, we mention only a few
whose work the student may find opportunity to study.
Braque's compositions are excellent examples of the use of
blacks, grays, and yellows. Marcoussis's flair is for pure and
intense harmonies in which black and white patterns and motifs give structure and unity. Ozenfant combines neutral
grays with pastel hues in severe geometrical pattern. One of
the greatest of modern colorists was the Spaniard, the late
Juan Gris. A study of his odd harmonies will reward all painters exploring the still uncharted realms of color. The originality of his conception and his imaginative resourcefulness
in composing will remain a source of inspiration to all workers in color.

In the United States, the art of color has made tremendous
strides through the efforts of the younger men in spite of
much organized official and social hostility to esthetic innovation. Abstraction is condemned generally because on the surface it seems divorced from the traditions of painting. Those
familiar with its motivations recognize the connection to Classical painting underlying the surface appearance. Whether
they admire it or not, they do not question its usefulness as
laboratory study in composition. Whatever the student's

ultimate ambition in painting may be, he will lose much if he closes his eyes to the remarkable achievements of modern artists in the composition of harmonies of color.

The absolute in color is being constantly sought. About two decades ago certain workers on the fringe of art, imbued with this desire and no doubt infected with the current phobia for scientific efficiency, contrived systems whereby the problems of art were to be easily solved. There are always great numbers of people who seize upon a system as a gift from Heaven. They advertise what benefits they have received from it when the truth is that the benefits derived are entirely psychological as in faith healing. The discouraging aspect of such faith healing in art is the victimization of many talented and important artists who would attain fame with or without theories, systems, and special materials. These men will endorse crackbrained profundities achieved by mathematics, systems of absolute color attained by spectral gradations, etc. In the case of the color systems only the hues of color receive attention from the inventors. The quality is with little exception grayed and opaque. In spite of this, some notable pictures have been painted with such pigment by exceptionally talented enthusiasts. The late George Bellows was a famous advocate and user of the infallible system. He taught his students from a scientifically prepared and graded palette, and wrote endorsements of a mathematical system of pictorial composition. But the truth is that Bellows was neither a composer nor a colorist, but a remarkably facile draughtsman and brushman. The scaled pigments which he used and recommended are to my knowledge no longer manufactured.

In short, to find a scientific short cut to color is to find a device for fathoming the personality. Such machines only succeed in flattening, not fathoming, the one as it does the other. The color of the artist is his mood, his emotion, his intellectual slant, his personality. No absolute exists.

There is only one way to arrive at a personal palette or even at an understanding of color and that is through ceaseless experiment in harmonies and dissonances. Odd colors should be prepared and tried in juxtaposition with black, white, and the prismatic colors. A good method is to prepare numerous charts, labeling each mixture and devoting individual panels to each new discovery in combination with a pure color, or with grays, black, and white. When a particular combination, as for instance a dull lemon yellow and a dark, matt gray, appeals to the painter, he may make a record of the effect for use in a composition.

The chart is an elementary exploration. It is only in the study of color in relation to design that a distinctive and personal palette reflecting the nature of the artist can be achieved. (Look up the montage designs of Kurt Schwitters.) Color composition means the juxtaposing and circulation of color in a picture in such a way as to create a single moving and appealing statement, in two dimensions and in three dimensions. The chart will be the lexicon for the statement. The construction of the statement itself is the subject of the following chapters.

PART II
THE PAINTER'S COMPOSITION

XII

INTERVAL AND DIRECTION

MOST PAINTINGS currently produced, and indeed most paintings in our museums, reveal little effort toward an intellectual synthesis, or the organization of the material as design.
This absence of composition is not proof that painting has
no need of the composer's art, but is evidence only of the
preference of past museum committees for surface painting, a
craft of skill rather than a product of intellect and imagination. We often use the phrase "fine art" to distinguish painting from advertising "art"; but if we were purists in speech
we should limit the use of the term "fine" to painting which
is dependent mainly upon its plastic qualities (essentially
the elements of composition) as distinct from painting which
is primarily a copy of nature, illustrative, anecdotal, sentimental, etc. By far the greater amount of painting put before us is not fine art in the sense here given; it is a product
not so far removed from commercial art as their authors believe it, since its superiority lies only in degree of competence,
not in any distinct elevation of the spirit.

Yet it must be acknowledged that many paintings lacking
composition may be worthy of the admiration of cultivated
persons. Such prized paintings resemble the great mass of
mediocre work in objective and procedure, but are distinguished by a quality of expertness markedly exceptional.
They are not the mere product of sensibilities and intelligent
command of craft but something beyond this equipment of

111

the competent painter, hence phenomenal. For want of exact diagnosis we call them works of genius. Three objections may be made to this order of genius. First, it leads to a vast amount of imitation by persons who do not possess genius and so results in a plethora of sterile canvases. Second, since skill constitutes its principal virtue, it is apt to be on the border-line of "tricksterism." Third, it falls outside the tradition of painting, leaves no deposit upon it, nothing for successive painters to build upon. The sum of these objections is that such art diverts attention from esthetic principles which if not eternal are almost universal.

There are two distinct arts in painting just as in music. These are the performance and the composition. In painting, unlike music, the one may exist almost entirely without the other. The performance may be in itself an enjoyable experience for the spectator—the brushwork may be superb, the drawing facile and sensitive, the color glowing and poetic. Such virtuosity is often admirable but is also overesteemed because of our weakness for hocus-pocus. In painting, as in music, performance has a time element, composition has not. Consider, for example, the decline in esteem of the virtuosos Zorn and Sorolla, not to speak of our own Sargent. We have need too of a kind of picture which is more of the mind and less of the hand; which does not call attention so much to how it is done as to what its creator felt; which subdues its means in order to emphasize its ends; which, instead of being made with magic, magically stimulates the spectator. For the intellectually inclined person only the composed picture will offer lasting satisfaction.

Satisfaction is derived from its principle of continuous activity and change. The magic which we feel is the magic of being led through a plausible but unfamiliar world, exploring its corners, returning again and again to the starting

point and seldom taking the same route. Thus the charm of
the picture is kept alive, its freshness constantly renewed.
Change or activity does not of course occur on the canvas,
but if the arrangement or design is good, a continuous movement and fresh viewpoint is induced. Our eyes are made to
move about the limited area in an all-encompassing, unifying
way, and variations in route are almost limitless.

Another way of stating the difference between the composed picture and the well-painted but not composed one is
through the much misused terms dynamic and static. In the
latter category the brilliantly painted passages scattered about
the canvas are independently noted. A canvas in which the
esthetic virtues are taken in order is a static thing, a collection of telegrams quickly read. Composition makes the painting dynamic, an active, organic thing. It is a principle or
device for confining the esthetic virtues of a canvas in such a
way that each points to a single statement within the boundaries of the canvas, in an ever-changing order or relationship. I shall try to demonstrate, in a necessarily elementary
way, how this is done. I shall not attempt to list every means
for arriving at orderly and organic presentation of material,
but only those major elements which can be explained by
black-and-white illustration. More desirable than a catalogue of methods and devices is the inculcation of an attitude.
The composer's principal need is the feeling for rhythm (action, pause, interval, direction), the elements of the dance.
The fine dancer may be his own choreographer, the good
composer of painting may invent his own means. (Proof of
this is the fact that almost every notable composer issues a
dogmatic code of esthetic laws and procedures. Witness
Propos d'Artistes of Florent Fels.)

The simplest unified statement pictorially is the silhouette.
If a silhouette is made, let us say of a cat, it is something more

than an outline of the cat; it is a spot or mass of black. If a margin is placed around it, a relationship is set up (as well as a contrast or opposition) between the black mass and the thin black line. When finally the silhouette is placed in a narrow black frame, there is added a further series of relationship-differences, the intervals of white as well as the intervals of black. We hang such a framed black and white because we consider it decorative, as it undoubtedly is.

The terms decorative and designed, as understood by the painter, are not synonymous but are on the contrary opposite concepts. Decorative treatment of an area is the breaking up of the area in such a way as to form interesting static divisions. A designed area is the treatment of the area by lines, lights and darks, and colors in such a way as to enhance the movement or rhythm of the entire picture. From this point of view our silhouette is not a design, it is merely a decoration.

The silhouette, in this case, is static. It is precisely the same as a conventionalized rendering of a plant form within a square in that the eye is taken immediately to the center and held there or else radiated out from the center (see Figure 15, *a* and *b*). This static effect is the very quality the intelligent painter wishes to avoid. If his picture is to possess any lasting value, it must have movement.

Using the same silhouette as illustration we shall try to make it a simple design rather than a decoration. We shall give it movement by placing it away from the center of the area so that the symmetry and balance are destroyed (Figure 15c). A disturbing disequilibrium requires that we balance the area with equally emphatic spots elsewhere. To place more cats in the area at equal intervals will result in a static piece of decoration not differing essentially from the first attempt (Figure 15d). But if instead of attaining a literal bal-

FIGURE 15

ance we select other patterns of black differing in size and shape and interval from our original cat, we may attain not an exact balance as of a man standing with legs spread but a movement in equilibrium as of a dancer poised.

Success in such unsymmetrical (occult) balance is dependent upon a cultivated taste for the exact interval. Each spot is related to every other, and what is equally important, to the edges of the area. If this were not so, the area would be incomplete; the eye must be kept moving within the boundaries of the area without the necessity of a frame to limit a wandering gaze.

As painting becomes less and less an art of design and more an art of realism, brushwork, modeling, etc., the painter contents himself with the barest requirements of the sense of interval to confine the spectator to the area of his canvas. Much use, for example, is made by unimaginative painters (and art school classes) of so elementary a device as the "crescent and star." The term should make the means apparent at once. If we place a crescent in a confined area the slenderness of its mass and the positiveness of its direction will create a disequilibrium which may be corrected by a point well placed with regard to the margins and crescent. Completeness is attained after a fashion, not artistic. It is a mechanism aptly illustrated by Joshua Reynolds' *Saint Cecilia* in which the light pattern made by the figure of Cecilia at the harpsichord is neatly balanced by the light pattern of the book of music. Such limited organization offers little more than a requisite stop to the eye and leaves the painting dependent upon its technical virtues and extraneous qualities for its appeal.

The notes which dominate a canvas are the lightest and darkest patterns. The eye moves from light to light and dark to dark and from one spot of color to another spot of the same color. (This selectivity of the eye is not a theory; experiments

FIGURE 14.—The charcoal drawing as preparation for the painting

FIGURE 16.—*Three Miracles of St. Zenobias by Botticelli*

have demonstrated that the eye seeks classification and order, the basis of rhythm.) To repeat, if the spots or patterns are equally spaced with regard to each other and to the edges of the area, the picture will be static. Instead of the intervals having the varied character of the steps of a dance, they will have the dull quality of the sentry's back-and-forth pace. It is the unequal disposition of dominant notes (compensated by variety of size, and emphasis, or by brilliance of color) which creates the dynamic picture.

The sense of rhythm as expressed by interval is older than the history of Western painting. We have the wonderful examples of Chinese drawings, the manuscript illustrations of Hindus and Persians. Closest in time and tradition to the beginnings of European art is the church painting of the Byzantines. These founders of Italian art combined the two basically different concepts of design and decoration. Their decoration is meticulous ornament almost Arabic in its abstract order and in its profusion. Their design is generally a symmetrical framework with enough disequilibrium to afford stress and accent. They used gold leaf not only to give a luxurious surface to their decorations but because the rich metallic note, more effective than mere color, offered a further means for the expression of interval. Thus the artist placed a gold halo about the head of a saint and distributed other halos at points necessary to the rhythm, with saints beneath to receive them.

Eastern sense of interval became the heritage of the Italians of the Middle Ages, particularly the Florentines. It reached its finest expression in the work of such artists as Fra Angelico and Botticelli. These composers, whose works have the quality of the ballet in their rhythm and impersonality, added to the sense of interval the sense of direction (as distinct from the design of line). That is, they made the pattern of dark or light carry the eye in a certain way. To explain this notion of direction further, the marks of playing cards—diamond, heart, spade, club—are geometrical variations of pattern but are identical in their direction, or rather, lack of direction. The card itself, however, is a rectangle which may be placed on the table in a limitless number of directions. An excellent example of such design of interval and direction is the composition of Botticelli here reproduced, *The Three Miracles of St. Zenobias* (Figure 16).

The symmetry of the plan is almost Byzantine but the use of dark pattern prevents the dissolution of the whole into the parts. Rhythm carries the interest throughout the area, making a single statement of man, horse, building. While each group is designed more or less as a pyramid, the darks in each pyramid bear relation to the darks of the canvas generally, being part of a system. The great geometrical variation in the patterns naturally adds to the movement of spot to spot. But this geometry not only gives interest to the patterns as such; it gives each pattern a direction. The figures are curved patterns inclosing the action. The patterns in the pilasters are vertical, those in the architraves horizontal. The diagonals expressing the perspective of the two buildings lead the eye to an important horizontal black which unites the two parts of the picture. Note that this horizontal pattern connects with the pattern of the horse, linking distance and foreground in another unity, that of the sense of space. (We shall look into this attribute of space more fully in another chapter.) The emphatic horizontals and verticals create a serenity and stillness like that of the financial district on Sunday morning. The huddled figures with their directionally varied darks create a dramatic contrast. The sense of excitement is heightened by a perfect note, the single sinuous

FIGURE 17.—Analysis of a painting by El Greco showing the Byzantine symmetry made dynamic by opposing diagonals

FIGURE 18.—*Design by Mondrian*

line made by the fluttering pennant. It is not only the fertile variety of the pattern (the windows are rectangular, arched and circular; the tree forms definite) which gives distinction to the picture but the contrast in interval creates a positive movement within the area of the canvas. The six black windows in the upper right are, in their regular beat, the castanets of the dance.

Before leaving the elements of interval and direction, I should like to call attention to an aspect of such design which is a matter of esthetics in a general sense. When Botticelli painted a miracle, or Fra Angelico the beheading of a saint, the emotion of the scene is filtered and transmuted by the style of the design or the art form. If I insist upon the words dance and ballet, it is because the composer's art in painting not only resembles these in its plastic elements but also in its psychological effect upon the spectator. We do not feel the horror of the beheading, we feel sympathy in a contemplative sense. We are not made to witness a re-enactment of the actual deed; we do not experience the clutch at the throat, the stilled heart, disquieting sensations of the stomach, or the tears starting to the eyes. These are the sensations of the theater, possibly of literature. When the painter solicits them, he is invoking extraneous means, he is an illustrator. The Romantic movement in painting which has captivated Europe and America since the Renaissance is, when it is really effective, theatrical. Not until the present century have painters attempted to restore the compositional elements of painting so that the spectator may be made to enjoy the subject matter *through* the art form rather than the emotions awakened by his participation in an emotional scene.

The theatrical painter uses light and dark not as patterns rhythmically placed but rather for their suggestive qualities.

Dark will represent mysterious shadow, light the revealing finger. The Romantic painter's use of light is precisely the same as the stage director's; he throws the spotlight upon the action leaving the vast areas of the darkened stage as a foil. He bids one sit in on the drama, weep with the mourners, exult with the victorious.

Such a composer (if we may term this order of presentation composition) was Rembrandt. In his *Woman Taken In Adultery*, the characteristics of his style are to be found. The vast stage of the temple is in deep obscurity while the important actors in the drama, very small and overwhelmed by the space about them, are illumined by a mysterious, shapeless light. It is a gleam which flickers, flares, and dies in the reflective surfaces of the great columns. Quite of the theater. The eye is quickly riveted to the focal point. The picture is dramatic, but unfortunately it is also static. Its invitation to the spectator to participate in the scene eliminates the art form because the emotions of the participant are very different from the emotion of satisfaction in the art form. We thrill to the music of Bach. We also thrill to the song of birds as we lie under the apple trees. But we do not demand that Bach's music thrill us in the same way that the notes of birds do.

There is in the history of art a singular and notable combination of the dramatic use of light in the Romantic manner and Classical design. This is the composition of El Greco. Byzantine geometry determines the order of his canvases, division of area and direction of line establishing the framework for the painting. But such dramatic impact is derived from the movement of the light that the geometry appears to be secondary. The lights shoot through his canvases like quivering tongues of flame. Great sweeps of dark line and shadow accentuate the restless and fervid movement. There is a very conscious direction in this movement of light and dark and this together with the distortion in drawing create the style which permits us to enjoy the drama, not as realism, but through the medium of the art form. See Figure 17*a* and 17*b*. (Note: Imitators of El Greco intent on copying his style miss the design. In consequence, style becomes mere mannerism as in frequently seen contemporary works.)

When we say that composition fell into desuetude after the Renaissance and remained ignored until modernists made the rediscovery, we do not mean that the program of modern art was to restore the painting styles of the Italians. There have been many idioms of painting since. It would be pointless to attempt to recapture a dead language. But the attitude to the picture as a consciously designed unit has been resurrected by modern artists. Some have pursued one element, some another. It is the intention here to show the new ways in which Classical elements have been isolated and made the basis for research and development.

With respect to the two elements we have so far described, interval and direction, it will be fruitful to the student to compare the experiments of the Belgian contemporary, Mondrian, with the picture of Botticelli. To the former, composition is nothing more than a division of space for interval and direction. The problem is made more difficult to solve by restricting possible patterns to rectangles, no two of which are alike. The reproduction (Figure 18) shows the form which the two compositional elements take as an abstraction. The esthetic validity of such painting is not for us to judge. It is left to each informed person, in the light of his own sense of values, to accept or reject.

XIII

DESIGN OF LINE

IT IS universally agreed that the good draughtsman is he who makes his line expressive rather than accurate. The Chinese of the fifth century and the photography teachers of the present are in accord on this principle. All that remains is for one to define what is meant by the term *expressive*. Expressive of what?

Two draughtsmen wish to express action, let us say the action of wrestlers. One makes a drawing of men in contorted positions, muscles bulging and strained, faces pugnacious and pained. The observer is made to feel the tremendous effort expended, also to admire the ability of the artist to express the story. The other draughtsman finds in the two bodies certain directions of line which oppose each other, certain conformations of pattern, a curve, sharp angle, graceful, fluid line. One line is light, another rather black. The combination of these varied qualities and patterns of line have the effect of making the eye move rapidly around the area. The lines express action. The first draughtsman, undoubtedly an admirer of Rubens and Delacroix, expresses action in the immanent (Romantic, theatrical) sense. The second expresses action in the Classical tradition of linear design.

The basis of all such design is geometrical variation. Whether the Classical artist pictures a riot or a tulip in a vase, his interest is the movement of line, organic rhythm. Thus a superb draughtsman such as Ingres, an expert in realistic

122

FIGURE 19.—*Portrait* by Gentile Bellini

FIGURE 20.—*Drawing of Ezra Pound by* Henri Gaudier-Brzeska

drawing, painted nudes in rhythmical contours which no model could possibly assume; but so skillfully that the design was not even seen by the professors of anatomy who admired his precision and accuracy.

For explanation of this principle of rhythm let us return to our most elementary diagram, the silhouette of the cat (Figure 15). The contour is one fluid line. It does well enough for purposes of representation since the soft and rounded forms of the cat suggest the use of such line (or vice versa). But from the viewpoint of design, it is meaningless. There is no interplay of geometry with its consequent appeal to the imagination and sense of order in movement. In Figure 15 e, the silhouette is changed into a spot drawing for the purpose of showing not only some variations of line possible in the contour but the relationship of such line to other lines within the contour. While this is necessarily a simple illustration of the idea, it will serve to make intelligible the motivations of non-Romantic draughtsmen. Witness such classical examples as the drawing of Gentile Bellini, an early Venetian painter. In his portrait (Figure 19) we are made to see first the simple geometrical volumes and pattern of body, arm, head, and hand. (The pattern of the hand is as abstract as a modernist's version.) Next we are made conscious of the rhythm of the line by means of the emphasis of dark—the accented spot of palm and fingers, the sharp stress of the edge of the tunic, the scalloped black around the head. It is the face, however, which is the terminal of the design. The severely geometrical patterns of eye, cheekbone, jaw, lips, and chin are not only interesting in relation to each other, but what is much more important, are planned in rhythm with the larger darks and lines of the ensemble. Observe the cheekbone alone with relation to the ovoid shape of the head, the line of the jaw with relation to the angle

made by the hat as it touches the jaw, the line and angle of
the raised hand and arm with relation to the direction of the
other arm. These are the more obvious rhythmical relationships. There is more to the design than such bare analysis
suggests (as, for example, the design of volumes, the subject
of another chapter), but it should suffice to show the artist's
intentions.

In contrast to this design in drawing there is the widely
known work of Holbein and Dürer. Accuracy of anatomy,
sensitivity of line, a highly cultivated technical precision distinguish the work of these northern artists. But the qualities
for which they are admired are remote from Classical consid-
erations of design. Realistic and Romantic drawing dates
back to the German masters. It has always been in the as-
cendancy, first because its appeal is immediate, second because the average cultivated person is responsive to technical
proficiency or craft. The notion of design, as distinct from
decoration, is not ordinarily inculcated, nor is it the ordinary
property of humans. It is something discovered and then
practiced, and relatively few in our present scheme of life
seem to have the need or desire to acquire it at the cost of
prolonged effort.

Modern painters who reject Romanticism and realism in
drawing select their models from the art of dead (or remote)
civilizations into which the sense of design was incorporated.
The paintings of the Chinese, Persians, Egyptians, Byzantines, and Italian primitives offer them rich examples. Spo-
radic rebellions against Romanticism crop out at odd points
in European history. David, the artist brought into promi-
nence by the French Revolution, defied the art of his Romantic predecessors, the court painters, and attempted to restore the cold design of the Italians. His most famous pupil
was the artist above mentioned, Ingres, a more talented, far

Achille Bouis, phot., Montauban. F. Jaubert, Sup.

FIGURE 21.—*Nudes* by Ingres showing geometrical design and rhythm

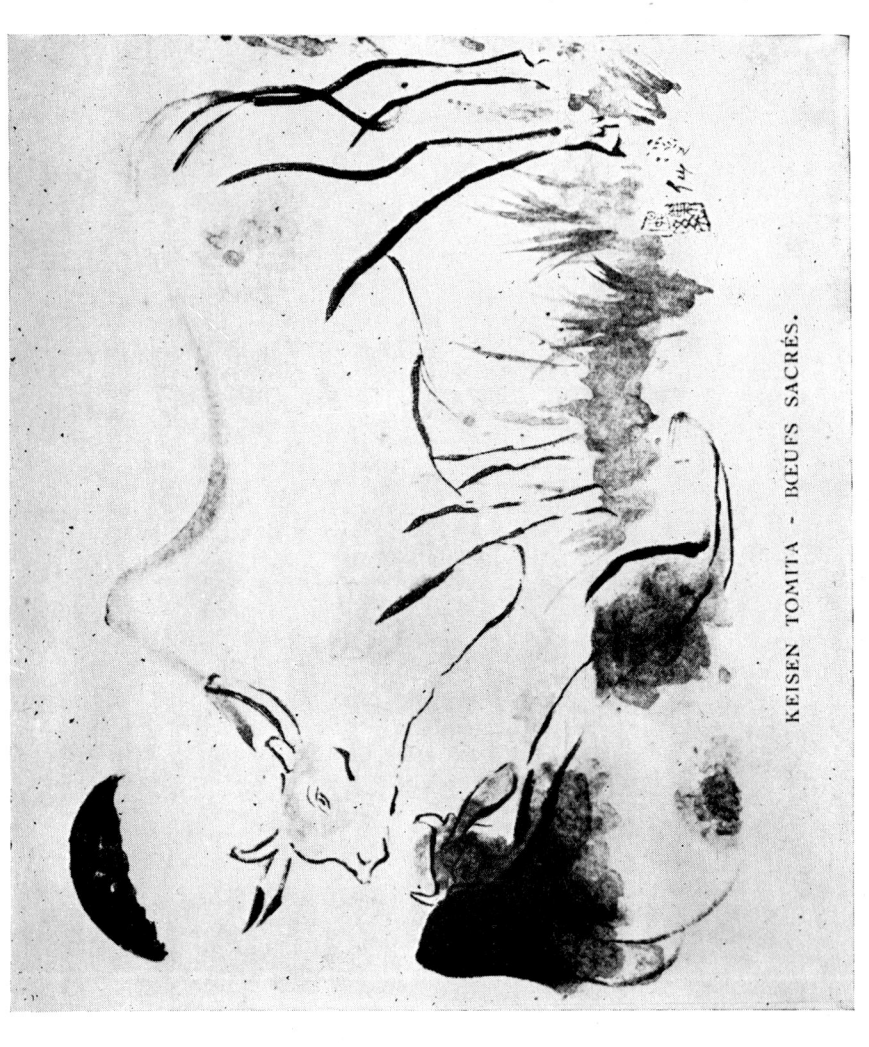

KEISEN TOMITA - BŒUFS SACRÉS.

Figure 22.—*Sacred Bulls* by Keisen Tomita

more compelling exponent of the Classical idea. French modern painters find in Ingres' linear design the seeds of Cubism,
so abstract is the mechanism underlying the apparently
literal contour.

Before studying an example of Ingres' drawing, let us
glance at a modern use of the principles employed by Bellini
in his portrait. We reproduce the sketch of a head made by
the late French sculptor Gaudier-Brzeska (Figure 20). Although expressed in a most modern idiom, its intentions,
structure, principles, are closely related to the Classical tradition. The play of fluid light line against heavy dry line,
the rhythmical repetition, use of decorative motifs as in hair
and eye, opposition of round to angular forms—all resemble
in intention the work of the early Italian. These elements
are the eternal interest of the Classical draughtsman.

Linear design for the painter is not restricted to the single
object or figure. It relates parts of a figure to the whole and
at the same time relates one figure to another so that the
entire area of the canvas is a series of line relationships.
Ingres' study of two nudes (Figure 21) shows how the artist
considers the geometry of one figure with relation to another.
The abstract configurations are obvious. Note, for example,
how the contour of the torso of the reclining figure is continued in direction by the line of the leg of the seated figure,
and the parallelogram made by the two legs. This abstraction
is made possible by suppression of literal contour and variation in emphasis of the different lines.

Most frequently the artist of line composition combines
his major interest with interval of spot. The drawings of
Orientals are such designs, as are most of the studies of modernists. The nudes of Braque are a play of incisive line
against an independent rhythm of gray smudge. In scattered
races unconnected historically, geographically, or anthro-

pologically, the fusion of line and spot for purposes of rhythm may be found. We reproduce two examples of such design, one the water-color drawing of a contemporary Japanese, Keisen Tomita (Figure 22), the other an Indian manuscript painting of the fifteenth century (Figure 23).

In Tomita's drawing the two spots of dark are balanced by the emphatic lines of the legs on the opposite side. The soft gray sweeping line of the back of the bull takes the eye in a swing from spot to black line. The thin scratchy line is made effective by occasional emphasis. Note the opposition of straight horn to round horn, the variations in the sizes and values (degree of dark) of the spots.

Turning to the Indian painting we find the same interplay of line and interval but in a more geometrical treatment. The division of the area for interval of light rather than dark creates the structure of the picture. This light design may well be examined. The upper third of the canvas is a light area. Below it in the center is the prominently placed white horse. Had the legs of this horse been painted white like the rest, all movement would have been stopped, the design would have been static. But the artist used the custom of coloring the horses' legs to permit a graceful movement (by means of the arched neck) to the other light patterns bordering the lower right margin. The repetition of the arc in the necks of the four horses also takes the eye down rhythmically to the group assembled to welcome the prince. The spectator is made to feel that a multitude is acclaiming the visitor when actually there are only thirteen persons depicted. The illusion of greater number is attained by the many very small light patterns in contrast to the large area in the upper section; and also by the variations in direction of line. (Circulation of color also contributes to this illusion of a crowd.) Observe how the action is then taken upward along the left margin, first by the dark pattern of the drum and then by the ingenious use of little sinuous blacks which are made to represent patterns of women's hair and head-dress. All activity of the figures is accentuated by the con-trasting quiet of the long horizontal lines and the geometrical spots of windows and doors in the white building. Note how similar to the Botticelli is the architectural treatment with respect to the use made of the many small arched windows. The quietude attained by simple rectangular division is well planned as a foil to the excitement of the triumphant arrival. Added activity as well as decorative quality is imparted by the long, admirably spaced candelabra.

The design so far pointed out may be called the structural design of the picture since each element combines with the other to create movement or rhythm. In addition to this func-tion the line is decorative, that is, it makes novel pattern. Note, for example, the simplified drawing of the figures in the foreground and the patterns which result from the placing of one figure in front of another. Note also the differences in pattern in gowns and saddles of the five horsemen, and the ornamental drawing of the horses' legs. The sharp division of the picture into the two areas of light and dark is made less abrupt by ending the horizontal two-thirds of the way across and continuing the direction a little farther up.

There is in this type of painting a completeness and melo-diousness which makes much of our very sophisticated but conventional painting appear by contrast prosaic and frag-mentary, a reduction of art to the status of craft. It is not the poetry of subject matter which is the legitimate poetry of painting. It is the artist's organization of his canvas. Cer-tainly more has been written about the poetic allegories of Botticelli, his conception of ideal womanhood, etc., than of his esthetic or plastic principles. Whatever may be said of his poetic feeling, the fact remains that countless others possessed an equally fine feeling but were unable to express it in the painter's medium. Botticelli's rhythmical line and interval reveal a plastic sensibility as distinctly poetic as his allegories. The same is true of the Eastern painters of manuscripts. The elements which impart poetry to the picture are the compositional means, the same elements which modern painters attempt to recapture through the condensed language of abstraction.

FIGURE 23.—Fifteenth Century Indian manuscript painting

FIGURE 24.—*Christ's Entry into Jerusalem* by Giotto (a composition of several geometrical masses)

XIV

GEOMETRICAL MASS

THE FUNDAMENTAL difference between Eastern and West
ern painting is the simulation by the latter of the third dimension. To express fantasies of the spirit the flat picture is
not only adequate, it appears to us more desirable. But to the
Latin painter even Heaven has dimensions; the angels, weight
and volume. Reality for the Eastern artist appears to lie in
a sense of order; for the Western artist it derives from the
physical and material. The first disposes his actors and objects in an order which is esthetically ideal. The second puts
an idealistic interpretation upon earthly things and creatures
by imitating their appearance with slightly glamorous variations. The development of European painting from its Byzantine origins proceeded according to conceptual differences
not only of epoch but of race.

The art of Italian primitives fell back before the science of
Leonardo and the amazing performances of the later Venetians. The liberation of the Italian from Oriental asceticism
brought forth an art which praised the beauty of the real
world and not the beautiful idea. The emphasis upon design
disappeared. The art of composition dwindled to the flimsiest
formulas. But in spite of the process of change, important contributions were made by artists in isolated instances adapting
the early design to the demands of three dimensional painting. These artists were in the historical stream but not carried away by the tide of Romanticism. They overlooked no

contemporary discoveries. In fact, their composition is based upon such discoveries; it is a geometry of masses in an architectural sense. But since terms sometimes serve only to confuse, we shall look at some examples of their art.

The painting of Giotto remains an amazing accomplishment, so far removed is it from the time of its production. Looking at it through the distance of six hundred years we see it now as a forecast of the evolution of Western art, and also as the principal impetus for change. A hundred years before the Renaissance, this painter concerned himself with the composition of volumes. A horse was to him not a flat pattern as the Persians painted it but a barrel form with cylindrical legs. A human being possessed weight. A building was more than a façade; it was a cube-like structure. The problem for him was to arrive at an organization of area that would take these realities into account without sacrificing interval, direction, and rhythmical line.

This problem was solved by Giotto in grouping his figures and objects in masses which were large divisions of the area. In his fresco, *Christ's Entry into Jerusalem* (Figure 24), the means are readily apparent. The two groups face each other. The group on the right is a simple pyramid. The arms of the kneeling boy start the movement upward, the lines of the backs of the figures take the movement down again to the base. (Compare these repetitious lines, each slightly different, with the rhythms of the horses' necks in the Indian painting, Figure 23.) On the left, the massing of figures and donkey is a more involved piece of design. Behind Christ the figures form a rectangle. But within this rectangle occur many interesting variations. The figure at the extreme left sets the design in motion. The arm creates an arc which is repeated by the arm of Christ. The cloak hangs at a diagonal which is part of a series of upward lines, the cloak of Christ,

Figure 26.—*Entombment* by Titian (an example of a composition of two pyramids)

FIGURE 27.—*Woman at the Harpsichord* (also called *A Young Lady at the Virginals*) by Vermeer (an example of design of volumes and of rectangles)

and the neck of the donkey (lower line) carrying the interest over to the other group, thus unifying the picture. The upper line of the donkey's neck sweeps upward to the apex of the right pyramid. It is the sense of expansion of the forms, of arms and bodies and heads, which gives a reality hitherto unknown. The volumes are held together in a geometrical mass in the same way that billiard balls are held together by the triangle. Just as the spherical volume of each billiard ball is felt in the mass, so each volume of Giotto's figures makes itself felt while remaining part of a rigid design.

To explain further the difference between the intention of flat design and that of spatial design, let us glance at the two diagrams below (Figure 25, *a* and *b*). In *a* we see three geometrical elements—a circle, vertical line, and obtuse angle. Together they are interesting in their interrelations though they are not suggestive of anything physical. In *b* on the other hand, the lines are used as the edges of planes and so while remaining interesting, also create the solid sphere, the volume of which is made effective by the plane behind it running away to the rear. *B* is not possible without a knowledge of, or feeling for, *a*.

As painting became more concerned with natural appearance and the science of light and atmosphere, artists intent upon plausibility ignored the flat geometry of their predecessors. The earlier Venetians attempted a compromise; the later, proud of their virtuosity, discarded all which might pass as an intellectualism. The whole reason for the art was forgotten in the pursuit of realistic illusion. Veronese, commissioned to decorate a villa, played tricks upon visitors to the villa by painting life size figures on the walls in startlingly realistic attitudes, as for instance, on a wall at the end of the corridor, the picture of a page boy looking out behind a half-opened door. But before the decline of painting from an art of synthesis to the craft of human photography, heroic artists attempted the compromise between idea and appearance.

Titian, for example, retained the art form, not in a severe geometry to be sure, but in an observance of mass. In his picture *The Entombment* (Figure 26), we find the Romantic style held within a Classical composition. The three figures supporting Christ are fitted within the two diagonals almost symmetrically. The pyramid thus formed conveys a monu-

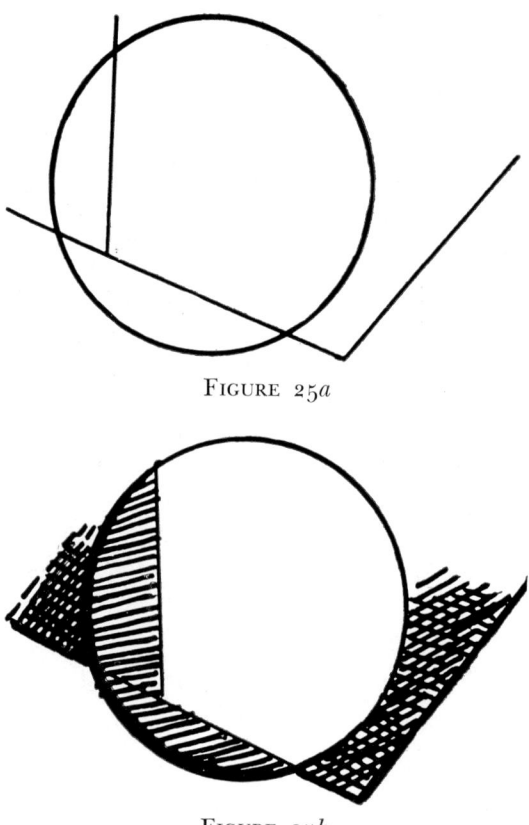

FIGURE 25*a*

FIGURE 25*b*

mental stability. It is true that it tends to "frame in" the central figure, and the artist therefore shifts our attention to the patterns of light of Christ's legs and arm rather than permit us to see the entire figure. And he eases our attention to the minor actors, the two figures on the left, by having them form a lesser pyramid. It is an effective arrangement but lacks the inventiveness of the Giotto.

The great masters of the north of Europe who looked upon the Venetians as Olympians came to study the revered masterpieces. They saw the way the texture of silk should be rendered and the transparent tints of flesh, but they ignored the structure of the painting. They took back with them much technical information but missed something of the esthetic principles. They wanted lots of life in their canvases even if the life was not organic in the picture but only a *description* of life.

There was, however, one great notable exception—Vermeer. His was the Classical spirit (phenomenal considering the social rôle Dutch artists played as picture makers for every bourgeois household). His work is as geometrical as the primitives, as exact in its sense of interval, and in addition possesses the weight and volume of Giotto's figures, the atmosphere and light of the Venetians. The geometrical divisions and masses in his canvas are so exact in their variations that no part of the canvas seems more or less interesting than any other, since each is meaningless without the other. His painting (Figure 27) is a piece of architecture which exists only by virtue of the relationships of the masses and patterns, not by any single focal point. Note the relative volumes of chair, body, harpsichord, head and arms, and the feeling of expansion which they engender in contrast to the flat rectangular patterns. (It is not difficult to see the relation between this design and the experiments of the modernist Mondrian, so exact is Vermeer's treatment of rectangles.)

Other Dutch painters painted much the same subject matter as Vermeer and attained occasionally a comparable quietude and peacefulness. But they depended upon an aerial and linear perspective to create that special charm of the Dutch interior. They lacked the ability to synthesize figures as volumes. Their interiors illustrate but do not give one the reality of the tactile sense nor the intellectual pleasure which comes in seeing fine organization of the canvas.

Geometrical mass as an element of composition is not as widely practiced by modern painters as it was a decade ago. The discovery of a new sense of space (which will be described in due course) is perhaps responsible for this decline. Nevertheless, there are many fine canvases extant which demonstrate the value of mass as a factor in composition.

An example of contemporary usage of mass is the reproduction of Gromaire's *Beer Drinkers* (Figure 28). The divisions of the canvas are geometrical and simple. The parts are either flat patterns or abstract volumes. The relations of these to each other are designed carefully. Note the right angle of the arm at lower left and within this angle the long diagonal of the body and the arc made by wrist and hand.

Gromaire's compositions are much more geometrical than Vermeer's since they treat the volumes of human figures as abstractly as the areas. They are in this respect closer to the painting of Giotto. But they are usually limited to two or three figures. It is therefore difficult to compare his methods more precisely with those of Giotto. However, if painting reveals at all the esthetic credos of the artist, it is no strain upon the truth to say that Gromaire's art belongs to the compositional tradition of Giotto.

FIGURE 28.—*Beer Drinkers* by Gromaire (design of volumes or mass in a modern geometrical style)

FIGURE 30.—*Eliezer and Rebecca* by Nicholas Poussin (an example of early space composition)

XV

SPACE AND THE SPATIAL RELATION

IN THE pictures discussed in the last chapter the illusion
of reality extends only to the objects or figures represented.
It may be asked what more could be done to secure this illusion. *The Entombment* of Titian startles the spectator by
the realness of the figures, so well are they modeled and
colored. But this verisimilitude is of wax figures before a
curtain. There is no *space* behind the figures, nor is there the
feeling of space between and around them.

In Giotto's paintings the figures are so simplified by the
geometrical style that we are made to feel, not their realness
as in the case of the Titian, but the *reality* of their weight
and volume. Behind them however there is likewise only an
ornamented back drop, not a world of volume and felt absence of volume.

The sense of space is not the same thing as the illusion of
distance. We may draw a few converging lines and the point
of their convergence may represent a distance of several miles.
The suggestion is made mentally by means of a diagram. The
statement is merely an answer, not a felt experience. We do
not in the course of travel relate distances to each other; we
merely accept the final report. If one wishes to know how it
feels to be in Alaska, it will not satisfy that wish to show, with
great pains, how Alaska is situated on the map. In the same
way perspective is unsatisfactory to the painter who wishes to
capture the feeling of space.

For this reason the great amount of research done by Ren

aissance painters in the science of perspective seems to us much wasted effort except in so far as its failures stimulated a few painters to pursue other means. Perugino secured a feeling of movement into the distance by simulating natural atmospheric change: the darks become lighter as objects and planes recede, the color more pearly until at the horizon all is lost in an indistinct bluish haze. His method of aerial perspective became a law of painting and with some isolated exceptions the only method of taking the spectator into the third dimension. Even today our academic exhibitions are full of pictures in which distance is suggested by the "fading-out" process.

The camera shows us how *realistically* Perugino caught the effect of recession. It also shows us that such recession is merely a statement in the same sense that the perspective diagram is, only it is in terms of values and color instead of in line. A photograph taken from the air which shows us a row of buildings, a river behind them, and another row of buildings on the other shore gives us the realism of the statement by making the second row of buildings very small, light and indistinct—the effect of perspective. We read in the third dimension in the same way we should read a string of objects—inventorially. For just as no relation exists between objects not arranged for design of line, so no relation exists between buildings, river, and buildings. There is a statement of distance, but no spatial relation.

Nicholas Poussin, painter in the court of Louis XIV, made a discovery regarding space which is as fundamental to modern composition as is Giotto's geometry of volumes. For him the removal of one object or area from another had significance only if a relation between the two were first established either by rhythm of line, or by interval, or by similarity and contrast in values.

I shall try to explain two of these principles by diagrams and then point them out together with the third in a reproduction. Figure 29a shows a building in the distance. In the foreground are two figures. They are designed in such a way as to create a rhythmic movement of line with the shadow which falls over the intervening area. The two planes are linked by this linear relationship.

Figure 29b shows two figures, one close to us, the other a

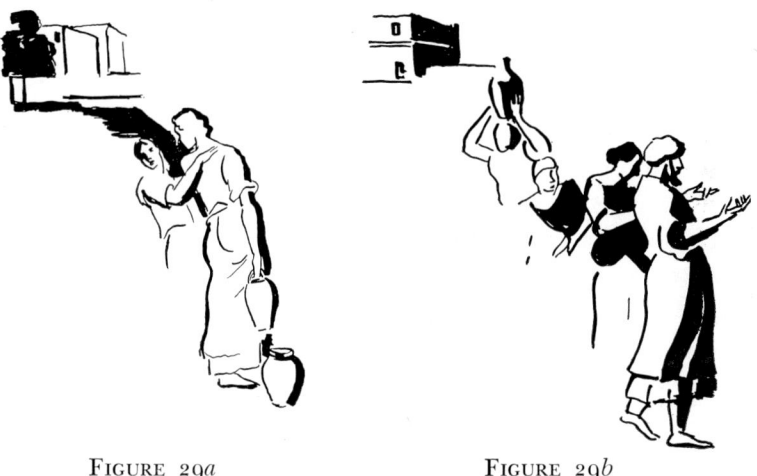

FIGURE 29a   FIGURE 29b

few paces removed. Still farther back appears a water jug balanced upon a head and in the distance a building. The volumes of the figures are suggested abstractly through contrasting patterns of light and dark. Note how interesting are the variations in their design, as for example the angular pattern of the woman, the curved line of the man's garment. Note also the repetitions in directions of arms of both figures (design of the ballet). Their significance is, however, not completely established until we see that the volumes of the figures attained through light on the left and dark on the right are repeated in the water jug and again in the building. These objects mark stages in the movement of recession. They establish a spatial relation. It is not, as some academicians might have it, the result merely of consistency in recording the natural laws of sunlight and shadow. If this were so, a half dozen other figures in the canvas in which these occur would partake of the same strong treatment of pattern; but the volume of some is scarcely felt. The repetition of value-pattern is used by the artist only to establish a sense of re-lationship at different spatial intervals.

The third principle, that of interval, will appear from a glance at Poussin's composition *Eliezer and Rebecca* (Figure 30). There are a number of water jugs in the picture but only two insist upon the spectator's attention because of their position and because of their modeling or volume. One is at the feet of the two principal characters, the other poised on the woman's head. If we glance from the first to the second and then to the stone sphere which rests on the column, a triangular relationship is set up which is most compelling since it is not merely a triangle on a flat piece of paper but one which has the magical quality of movement in the third dimension. One leg of the triangle runs away from us, another toward us. The relationship and the change in space are simultaneously established.

It will be apparent that the diagrams used above were taken from this painting. Therefore, no further analysis will be offered beyond calling attention to the application of the first and second principle *together* in another part of the picture, the extreme left. Here the light pattern moves to the urn and then back to the light rectangle of the dis-tant building. Only two planes are represented by these patterns, one near and one distant. Yet the effect is one of gradual movement backward attained not only by the pattern-

FIGURE 31.—*Houses* by Picasso

A modern example of space composition: the cubist method of planes in recession.

FIGURE 32.—*Spanish Landscape* by Eisenschütz

Another modern example of space composition: the abstract use of line and value-patterns

value but by the linear design, the variation. The double way of seeing this movement of light is of particular interest to the modern painter, as we shall see later.

While Poussin's classical composition has held the admiration of connoisseurs since its appearance, the spatial design which he created has been generally overlooked. It remained for modern painters to discover his gift for composing in the third dimension.

Watteau, who followed Poussin closely in time, attempted another solution for the problem of movement into the distance. His method was the alternate variation from warm to cool color in successive passages. Whether he was the first to discover this property of color contrast is not known; he is generally credited with the achievement. It is a major step in the history of painting as will appear from a comparison of color usages.

For Poussin, color was merely ornament. He expressed space through rhythms of values and line and colored the parts of the picture to make them appealing. For Watteau the color itself expressed space; it is not decorative, it is functional.

Decorative color in a picture is attained by putting together patterns of colors generally appealing in themselves and made more appealing by their relationships; for example, violet next to green. When Van Gogh in painting his bedroom picture in cool greens and blues placed a brilliant vermilion coverlet on the bed, he was striving only for a forceful decorative effect. The vermilion, not integrated in the composition, is just a statement which stimulates the eye. Gallery oracles will often exclaim at the beauty of a picture's color when what they mean is that the colors are in themselves bright or pretty, or that the tonal bath of the picture, the colored atmosphere which holds the canvas together, is tender or reminiscent of a particular mood of nature as when a setting sun reddens an erstwhile prosaic world or a twilight pallor lends a contrary enchantment. Tonality, unlike strong contrast, is sometimes an art in the manipulation of color; but neither is an art of color composition.

It is true that decorative color may also be incorporated in color design. The Eastern painters of miniatures and manuscripts did precisely this. Their colors are beautiful in themselves, more particularly in their imaginative combinations. But what gives them greater significance is the manner in which they are distributed for rhythm. Color was for these artists an art of interval as light and dark were for the Italians. A red spot at one point is repeated in a slightly varied red at another, and a third pattern subtly different in hue or mass creates a rhythm. Other colors travel in similar, but independent, orbits. Thus there results an interweaving of colors which imparts movement, in an abstract sense, or in a psychological sense, since the eye seeks notes of repetition and is carried speedily through the complex whole. This type of flat (two dimensional) color composition, while incorporating decorative color, is far removed intellectually from the merely decorative picture. It has the dynamic quality which the latter lacks.

The great achievement, which more than any other work created the directions of modern painting, is the color composition of Cezanne. Using Watteau's means to build upon and equipped with a far more effective range of color (the prismatic colors of Impressionism) he devoted his life to the reality of space and volume through color. So much has been written about this painter, so many reproductions circulated that there is no need to do more than summarize his methods. In the chapter on still life the design of the color-pattern was discussed. It is noteworthy that as the painter aged, his interest in this plastic element was superseded by a kind of painting which eliminated effective color pattern. He dropped local color and attempted to paint only the positions of planes. Where Poussin, for example, painted a house with one wall light and another dark to create the volume, Cezanne painted all planes of the house with warm and cool color and the area surrounding the house in the same way. Color as a decorative element was completely discarded. Its new service to painting was to give the illusion of movement through space and around volume. Just as local color was avoided, so was the strong value contrast. All colors to all surfaces, no strong darks and lights except for rhythm—these seem to be the strictures of Cezannism.

Essentially, such painting is an abstraction. It is the reality without the realness of the scene. It is not just an intellectualism because our senses are made to feel the volume and space. But the step from this appeal to the eye to an intellectual appeal of a theory is very close—and was inevitably taken.

Cezannism became the earliest phase of Cubism. We reproduce a picture by Picasso painted in 1909 (Figure 31). Here is a composition of houses in which the sense of movement is set up by means of varying directions of planes. There is no light and dark pattern but much light and dark rhythm. (There are no strong variations in color either.)

Compare this composition with the reproduction of the landscape by the contemporary Austrian painter Eisenschütz (Figure 32). In this landscape the methods of Poussin are revived. The sharp patterns of dark and light create the spatial relation. The rhythms of line connect the planes, the values separate them. In Picasso's picture the planes are in fusion, or even confusion, the deliberate aim of the painter having been to establish subtle relationships of space rather than a clear recession into the distance. In the other landscape the intention is to establish the volumes of the buildings in an unmistakable order (architectonic).

A later theory of space grew out of the Cubist experiments with the diagonal. It was felt by some painters that the elimination of patterns of color resulted in an arid canvas. Functional color was interesting enough but its subtlety eliminated the pleasurable sensations which painting of other times evoked. The question was asked, Why could not color be beautiful as well as functional? and great colorists prepared to produce a positive answer.

FIGURE 33*a*   FIGURE 33*b*

It was found that the diagonal direction of the plane compelled a spatial feeling without depending upon the color. The color could therefore be decorative. It was also found that color itself had properties of volume and space and that a spatial composition could result from a correct use of these properties. Let us consider the first discovery, the effect of the diagonal plane. If we take a number of blank rectangular cards and place them on the table at varying angles as in Figure 33*a*, recession is suggested; further, if we place vertical volumes upon these cards, the spatial intervals can be clearly determined (Figure 33*b*). And when in addition

FIGURE 34.—*Still Life* by Fresnaye (a beautifully organized space composition)

FIGURE 35.—*Partie de dames* by Henri Matisse (an example of equivocal space)

movement of line and interval are integrated in the composition, we have the reality of the third dimension expressed through geometrical design. The color may then be arbitrary.

This may be seen in the work of one of the rarest composers of our generation, the late Roger de la Fresnaye. In his still life (Figure 34) there is remarkable order attained through the exact interval of light and dark patterns and the rhythmical movement of line. The diagonals create a continuous movement, the oppositions of the axes of the planes leading the eye to the dark square which creates a necessary terminal. The circular lines make the composition organic by relating the directions of the many planes. It is interesting to note that Fresnaye's paintings are always effective in black and white, yet he was one of the foremost harmonists of modern art.

The properties of color which effect the spatial illusion are luminosity and depth. A luminous color has an expansive force; it reaches out from the plane behind it if this second plane is dark; even more effectively if it is of a complementary hue. For example, a brown building against a gray sky. The volume of the building can be expressed by two sides, one light and one dark. Where the dark side touches the sky, the gray may be made warm to receive the brown. But the light side will be in stark opposition to the sky by being made a luminous warm yellow plane against a cold but non-luminous sky. The warm color of the building thrusts it forward from the cool sky. The luminous plane of the building gives the illusion of turning the building from light into the shadow. Thus the volume of the building is expanded and made effective not only by the hue but by the quality of luminosity of the color.

To set forth further examples of the modern usages of

functional color is to risk plunging the student into a morass of theories.[1] Here the intention is only to show the painter the possibilities which lie in the little known properties of color as agent in the attainment of space.

[1] Many theories for the sure attainment of space are offered by professors and painters. So distinguished a painter as Juan Gris advocated the use of color as demanded by the expansive (round) and restrictive (triangular) forms in a composition, disposing luminous colors to the first and dark opaque colors to the second. Ozenfant and Jeanneret together with their fellow Purists believe that every color has universal emotional stimulus and advocate a restricted lexicon of colors to express the painter's mood. Certain professors of modern painting have created the most involved science of the tension of planes and the color demanded by these tensions. For me these are all recipes—more interesting when given out by good chefs than by mere theorists, but suspect even then because the chef does not include his talents and experience (not to speak of personality) in the typewritten list of exotic ingredients.

POSTQVAR CONSVMATI SVNT DIES OCTO VT CIRCVCIDERET PVER VOCATV E NOM ET IHES. LVCE. II. C

ELONGAVI FVGIENS 7 MANSI INSOLITVDINE . PS . XXXXXV . C

SVRGE ACCIPE PVERVM 7 MATREM ET 7 FVGE INEGIPTVM . MACEI . II . C

FIGURE 36.—*Flight into Egypt* by Fra Angelico (a Renaissance use of rhythm for equivocal space)

FIGURE 38.—*Still Life* by Juan Gris (an example of equivocal
space in abstract art)

XVI

SPACE IN ABSTRACT ART

AT THIS point we arrive at the most radical departure from traditions of Western painting. Through a long process of experimentation, painting succeeded in becoming three dimensional. The modern revival of interest in composition led to an exploration not only of the Classical elements in all periods of our art but to a search for eternal truths, universal laws. Negro, Egyptian, Byzantine, Chinese, Persian art have been examined and analyzed. The influences of all these forms may be traced in the works of prominent painters. In the course of this search and recapture a discovery of tremendous importance was made, that of a new sense of space. Henri Matisse is generally credited with this discovery.

This new sense of space is not a space suggestive of a new dimension such as higher mathematics visions. It is new only in the quality of its illusion. It is made by combining the two dimensional view with the three dimensional. The spectator sees an object or area in one way one instant, in another the next. He has the sensation of seeing double or of seeing contradictory statements. The term given to this illusory effect is *equivocal* space.

Equivocal space is a rediscovery, rather than a discovery of modernists. Evidences of it are to be found in such Classical composition as that of Poussin, more frequently in the design of Fra Angelico, as we shall see. Its origins, however, are much older, dating to the manuscript paintings of the

145

Persians. Matisse denies that he borrowed the idea from these paintings. We can only do as the newspapers do, that is, say in large black headlines, "Matisse denies influence."

What characterizes Persian art, aside from its beautiful design of rare color and line, is the quality of its story. The story is made into fantasy by deliberately separating object and pattern. To grasp this, imagine two passages of color, one red the other green. Now some colors or luminosities have the property of nearness, others of remoteness, as we have seen. If the red appears near and the green far, there is obviously a spatial difference. If then we draw the outline of something, let us say of a horse, to cover the two passages of color, we have the disturbing sensation of seeing the horse as an entirety at one moment, and at the next seeing him divided in two, half of him nearer to us than the other half. It is a fairy tale element expressed plastically. There is no doubt that such illusion was deliberately sought by a people notable for their imagery and fantasia.

Sometimes, however, the requirements of the pattern or movement of light will demand that the artist separate the values or colors of an object. In such case there may result, quite accidentally, an equivocal sense of space. To see a clear instance of this turn back to the Indian painting. In the lower right corner the body of the horse is kept within the light pattern, the head of the horse in the dark pattern. The horse appears headless. When the German painter Campendonck or the Russian Chagall deliberately cut off the heads of cows and put them in different spatial planes they were striving for the fantasy of Eastern art.

The same confusing (but charming) effect is attained by a profusion of ornamental motifs. If a distant area is ornamented and a near one equally ornamented, the eye will note the two areas as on one plane. This is the device which has been the specialty of Dufy and Matisse. Dufy follows more closely the Persian fantasy, quite content with the element of fancy which he is able to recapture. But Matisse attempts a combination of European modeling (realistic volume) with the Oriental profusion of ornament. Thus he increases the confusion. He puts before the spectator a scene in which the parts seem real but their relationships impossible or ridiculous. See for example his *Partie de dames* (Figure 35). The woman is seated at the piano, but the piano appears to be floating in the air. This is because of the white stripe of the rug which links white figure and white ornamented wall in one plane. Examined further the woman appears to be sitting on top of the figure at the table in the foreground. The floor on the right side appears to be a vertical rather than a horizontal plane because of the cross-hatching. The profusion of ornament throughout destroys any possibility of a convincing architectural order.

While Matisse may have been the first painter of our day to point attention to the possibilities of equivocal space, it is questionable whether he has put the discovery to the best use. If the objective is to create an added element of movement, to make the picture dynamic in its depth, is not this objective destroyed by the very monotony of its means? It seems to us equivocal space is desirable only when it is structural in the picture.

An example of what is meant by structural use of such space is to be found in the composition of Fra Angelico, *Flight into Egypt* (Figure 36). Here the illusion is created not by ornament nor by the device of breaking an object into two spatially different colors but by the movement of line. The line swirls about the picture in rhythmical directions. It also passes from a distant area into a near area uniting them in one plane when seen abstractly. For example, note the contour of the hill on the right. It descends to a point about two fifths of the way from the top and swings suddenly into the direction of the leg of the riding figure. Not only does the line have this direction, the volume of light of which it is only the contour moves into the light volume of the leg. Distant and near volumes make a single rhythm on one plane. Looking back into the picture we note that the sharp angle made by the roof of the house is attached to a line representing an area far behind the

FIGURE 37

house and so both areas are linked in one plane. In the foreground we note the leaf-like pattern around the walking figure. The figure is so evenly placed in this pattern that the pattern gives the illusion of enveloping the figure and so is in the same plane, just as the halo is. There are further examples in this composition but since they are all attained by the same means we shall pass over them.

Note that the last part of the analysis of Poussin's composition deals with the same confusing illusion. The light rhythm is in one spatial plane, the objects which make it, in two.

This use of a single direction to express differences in spatial planes is much used by a group of modern painters who term themselves Purists. Painters like Ozenfant will attain the illusion of equivocal space by such line as in the drawing on the preceding page (Figure 37).

One line is made to express a contour of two objects, one near the other farther back. A further equivocal illusion is made by the dark passage which, while identical in the object and outside the object, comes closer to us in that part of the passage which is in the area outlined.

One of the most remarkable abstractionists to use equivocal space effectively was the late Juan Gris. Perhaps more than any other he succeeded in fusing into one small area the many elements of composition which have been described. In his still life (Figure 38) the sense of interval is very exact, the three white areas being perfectly placed with relation to the black. The diagonal thrusts of planes create the spatial feeling. The line design is a symphony in itself. This may be profitably examined here even though our interest at the moment is in the illusion of space.

The fluid contour of the goblet is described by the same line which gives shape to the pears. If there were no other lines in the picture, this one would be merely interesting. But in contrast to the severe white lines to the left, and to the two round lines which make a figure three on the right, the effect is comparable to counterpoint in music. Each line has a different tension, each complements the other, all together are fused into harmonious effect. In addition to this linear harmony (opposition) there is a linear rhythm which unifies the parts of the picture and repeats the theme. The rigid white lines are repeated in the lower edge of the table, the thick lower half of the figure three is repeated in the right shoulder of the bottle. The elliptical forms are also repeated so that the thematic character of the group of objects on the table is clearly felt. The restrained gamut of color serves to bind the various patterns together to permit the rhythm to function more forcefully than if disturbed by clashing, brilliant areas.

We turn our attention now to Gris' treatment of space. By the slight modeling of the pears the upper one is made to recede from the lower one. Back of them is the wine bottle. Behind the wine bottle is a black rectangle. In front of all this is the wine glass. So far the spatial relations follow those of the group in nature. But the world of poetic fantasy soon intrudes. The left half of the table top appears to be much farther back than the right half. Horizontal stripes on the dark screen continue across this plane of the table with no break, denying existence of space. The right vertical edge of the dark screen cuts into the table as if it were closer to us instead of more remote. The dark pattern on which the base of the wine glass rests appears to recede behind the lower left corner of the black screen. With all this obtrusion and recession the upper right corner and right side of the picture generally appear to be far behind the spatial activity of the group itself. All is confusion, yet all has the logic and simplicity of a wish.

Indeed such ventures into unreal space are of the quality of dreams. There is something mysterious and even thrilling in visual experiences which deny accepted physical laws. When we have such experiences, we term them hallucinations. But the modern painter, tired of recording and reporting, anxious to express poetry in non-literary terms, deliberately sets out to make such hallucinations. If he did nothing else but make fantastic statements, however, we could not take his work seriously (as in some of the canvases of Matisse). But when he imprisons his dreams in a structural form, im-

FIGURE 39.—An exercise in interval

FIGURE 40.—A synthesis of line and interval

parts to them a logical order and precision as inexorable as geometry, then we must acclaim him as a true composer in plastic art.

Whether or not we are emotionally touched by such art as that of Gris is of course a personal matter. (Many persons have no use for Wordsworth or Keats either.) The significance of the experiment to artists struggling with problems of design and space in any kind of painting is much more important than questions of prejudice. There is not only something to be gleaned from the study and analysis of abstractions, there is much more to be discovered from firsthand experience in the making of them. To learn to combine forms, grasp the vital structure of the picture, exercise the imagination in synthesis of unusual color harmonies, there is no better exercise than abstraction.

XVII

EXERCISES IN MODERN COMPOSITION

THE FOREGOING chapters on the elements of composition do not by any means exhaust the subject. But they will serve their purpose if the painter is moved by the examples given to attempt to present his material as an organic thing. It will be observed that the basis for all the elements described is geometrical. If there is any fundamental opposition between nature and art it lies in this quality of geometry.

In line with the method employed throughout it is suggested that the amateur painter experience first hand the processes discussed. The elements of design may each be made the basis for a separate study. In this chapter some exercises are suggested which should compel the student to find the means for the expression of desired objectives.

First come the qualities of interval and direction. A good exercise is one based upon Mondrian's paintings. Working in charcoal divide a rectangular area by horizontal and vertical lines into smaller rectangles, no two of which may be alike. All lines should extend from edge to edge. In three of the areas distribute three blacks in such a way that an unsymmetrical balance will result from the unequal interval. See that the blacks are varied as much as possible in size and are not all in one direction. (One black area may be horizontal, the other two vertical.) Distribute three or four whites in the same way but independently of the blacks. The remaining areas should be made light gray and dark gray.

No pattern should form a right angle (run in both horizontal and vertical directions); every pattern should be a rectangle unlike any neighboring one in value (Figure 39).

Translate the drawing into color. Choosing a color scheme of three hues, for example, red-brown, yellow-brown, and cold green, paint each black area a dark value of each color. Then do the same with the white areas distributing the color in an orbit opposite to the first. That is to say, a light green near a dark red-brown and so on. The color for the intermediate values will be determined by the demands of balance in the picture. Great variety in the sizes of the patterns and dynamic distribution of darks and lights are essential to the success of this exercise.

An excellent approach to linear design is through synthetic picture-making. This may be done first in charcoal. Distribute through a rectangular area a number of lines of different length, quality, and direction. Oppose one diagonal movement with another, a curve to a straight line, a severe line to a fluid one. When there seems to be sufficient interest in the movement of line through the area without excessive pull in any one direction, distribute darks and lights exactly as in the first exercise. Close the lines into patterns arbitrarily so that the darks and lights will have definite boundaries. Add the intermediate values, again as in the previous study. Such a procedure will in almost every case result in an abstraction which suggests a picture (Figure 40). Developing this suggestion will of course depend upon the visual imagination of its maker. If the subject matter suggested can be given reality without sacrificing the interval and the interesting movement of the line, the study will result in a really valid painting. This incidentally was the method used by Juan Gris in arriving at his beautiful still-life compositions.

It is often asked why modern painters concentrate upon still life as subject matter for their paintings. The reason is that still-life objects have the greatest geometrical variety of form. The guitar of Picasso is much the same thing as the line of beauty of Hogarth. The crenelated edge of the Cezannian fruit bowl is the fluid line necessary to offset the precise geometry of oranges or pears. In other words, there are more abstract elements to be found in still life than in nature.

This brings us to another exercise: a still-life painting in which emphasis is put upon the rhythm of line, the line being abstracted from the collection of objects (the crenelated line from the fruit bowl, or the serrated edge from the saw). The line may be strengthened by black or neutral color in those places which are vital to the continuous movement. Indeterminate darks or smudges may be used to enforce the rhythm.

Drawing from the nude is of course the best practice for the cultivation of a sense of design of line. The body suggests the directional oppositions and rhythms but the draughtsman must select the precise kind of line with which to render them effectively. A line of equal pressure is a monotonous line. Thickness, thinness, rigidity, fluidity, grace, force—all these are expressive means for a rhythmical drawing. Brush and ink are particularly suited for such practice. The spot may be combined with line to effect a balance as in the illustrations shown in the chapter dealing with this subject. Another method of drawing from the nude is that favored by Braque. He uses a light gray smudge not to express anatomy as a literal copyist might, but to create a rhythmic movement which has meaning only in relation to the quick relaxed contour (Figure 41).

In painting the nude, the disposition of the areas sur-

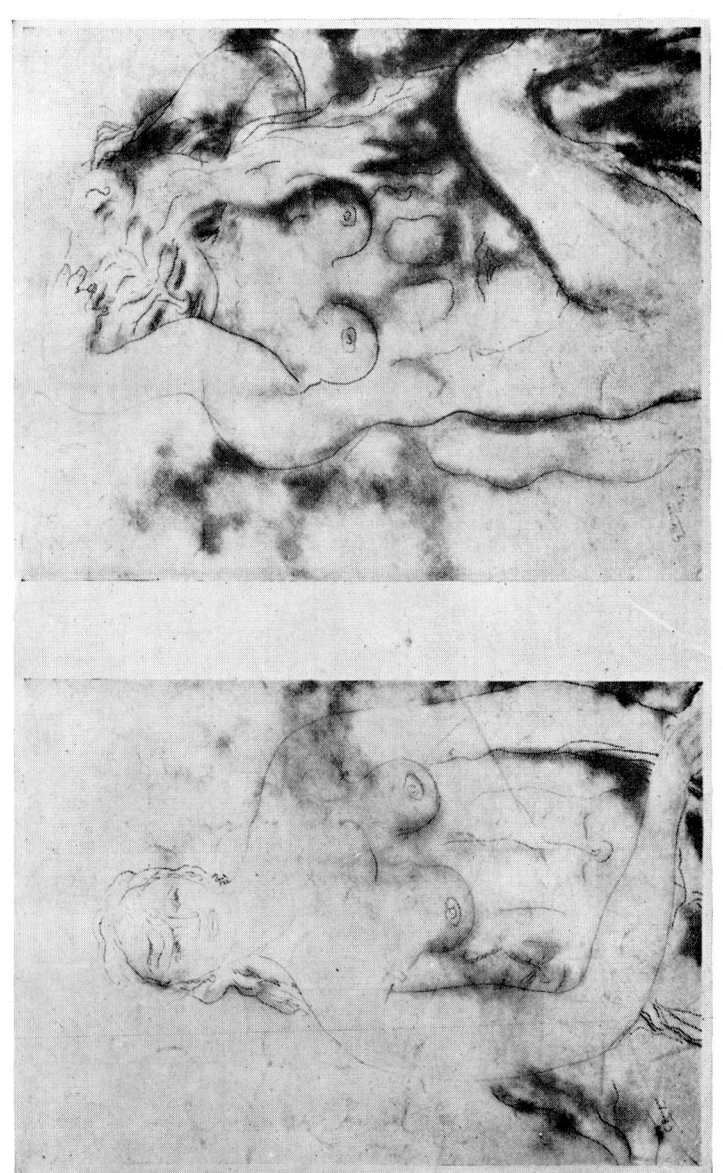

FIGURE 41.—*Nudes* by Braque (smudge and line combine to give an abstract interest to the area)

FIGURE 42.—An exercise in geometrical mass

rounding the figure should be dependent upon the directional lines of the figure both for opposition and for repetition. For example, if an arm makes a particular angle, the angle may be repeated elsewhere in the canvas; but a more important consideration is the opposition to it made by neighboring patterns. Sometimes the contour of the figure may not provide sufficient interest with relation to surrounding pattern of line. In such cases a form within the contour may be so treated that it is seen more readily than the line of the contour. For example, the lower leg when seen from a particular angle may present a contour of curved lines in an area where the artist feels the necessity for a severe vertical line. By stressing the line of the calf muscle against the shin the desired line is attained. The painting which makes as much use of such inner contours as of outer ones is apt to be much more rhythmical and better unified with the surrounding areas.

For an exercise in geometrical mass, take a painted pattern such as the synthetic composition made for linear design, and attempt to create volumes within simple geometrical divisions. The pattern will, as has been said, suggest still-life objects or human figures and the student should develop the suggested forms by planes, adding one or two, not enough to destroy the unity of the large simple divisions (Figure 42).

The compositional element which will hold the attention of the painter for many months is that of space. Here several exercises are suggested. The first is the arrangement of the area in dissimilar patterns in which the diagonal planes predominate. This will resemble the illustration of the cards placed at different angles. On different levels or elevations place a cone, cylinder, and cube. Arrange dynamic intervals of light and dark, some of them within the objects, some outside. Have a definite division between the horizontal areas (table-line) and the vertical areas of the background. Paint the diagonal planes in alternate warm and cool colors, not too decided in hue, reserving bright or luminous colors for objects, and areas surrounding objects. The object must be made to belong to the plane upon which it rests. This may be done by losing the dark side, let us say of a red object, in the red-brown of the area under it; of a green object, in the blue of the area, and so on. Each object should thus be separated by color from the other. Intervening areas should be neutral. If these suggestions are followed and the intervals of light and dark made dynamic, the resulting study should be expressive of the spatial relation.

A variation of the above problem is a synthetic landscape in which are three red buildings in different spatial planes, and three green hills. All other areas (sky, roads, etc.) should be neutral in color. Each hill should be given volume by planes, yet the greens used in each must be different in hue or quality from the greens in the other. The reds should also be varied. Instead of making the color fade as it recedes, paint the brightest red in the building farthest back and make the surrounding color hold it in its proper place.

Another variation of this problem of space is a (vertical) composition of a city street of tall cube-like buildings. Since most of the lines will be vertical, horizontal, and diagonal, interest may be added by designing clouds in round or fluid lines and by having the street curved, or by an elevated structure running through and connecting the buildings by curved lines. The problem is to make each cube take its place architectonically in the picture. This is a matter of planes of color and the treatment of contours. Luminous planes will be thrust forward, dark ones made to recede. The light plane will have a sharp contour, the dark one will

PLATE VI.—An exercise in still life abstraction

have a subdued contour. One building will be cool, another warm. This is not a simple exercise but it will reward the painter by an invaluable knowledge of the properties of color for functional use.

A problem combining two of the above exercises is a figure composition of three nudes or bathers on rocks. The rock forms will involve space through functional color and volume. The figures should be so designed as to be part of the line movement of the entire area. The color in the figures should likewise be circulated throughout in planned interval. The volumes should be expressed in only two values, designed patterns of light and dark. Such simplification in modeling will aid the unity of the picture since the rock forms will also be painted in simple planes. Caution: If the design in the drawing of the figures is restricted to the outside contours, the figures will appear to be silhouetted against the background, like actors before a backdrop. But if the bodies are so designed as to create patterns which may be repeated in the landscape, there will result an integrated and unified composition. This is a most complex problem and is in its essentials a summation of the principles upon which the preceding exercises are based. (See Plate VI)

Finally there is the exercise in equivocal space. This should be a fine synthesis generally. Still life is the most pliable subject. All the elements discussed should be incorporated in the composition, and the color should not only be functional, it should be fresh, inventive, everything which the academic painting is not. Use a color occasionally to express two planes, one near and one far, one in an object and one outside the object. The illustration in color (Plate VII) shows such an exercise. Note that the shadow of the orange bottle serves also as shadow for the green bowl in the foreground; that the orange color of the box becomes brown at the edge and passes into a similar brown in the background.

All of the above exercises have been used with good results in my composition classes. While they do not constitute a "course," they are comprehensive enough to give the student the idea of present-day composition. This idea he will develop in his own way and thus the inculcation of the design attitude, fundamental with the good painter, will have been begun.

PLATE VII.—Figure composition

XVIII

CONCLUSION

THE PRINCIPLES set forth in the foregoing pages will not be summarized for the reason that they are offered, not as a complete text like a rule-book of grammar or a manual of bookkeeping, but only as the facets of a point of view. Nor is the credo of the author offered as an infallible one for adoption by the reader. It is intended only as guidance in the selection of aims from which the individual's point of view may be shaped. The conviction earlier expressed, that the pleasure in painting arises from the challenge of clear objectives is, otherwise stated, the conviction that the painting of our day, to be an absorbing activity, must be motivated by an intellectual attitude.

The reader-painter comes to the end of this book without having reached a destination other than (it is hoped) a viewpoint. There is no other destination in art. Nor is there any final authority. The direction pointed out and the guidance offered have as warrant only the author's past successes in leading beginners through the several initial stages of painting to a capacity for making original pictures. If the material here presented succeeds only in awakening in the adult the ambition to discover for himself a satisfying cultural activity, then the book has justification enough.

Some advice on further study may be offered in parting. The custom of visiting contemporary or modern galleries should be postponed until the student has familiarized himself with the traditional schools of painting and the natural outgrowth of one from the other. The museum is, or should be, intended to supply this background. Unfortunately only a few of our museums possess well-organized or representative collections. Nearly all are the legatees of private collections expressing the confused tastes of wilful millionaires. Even the priceless collections in our great museums will confuse the serious student by the conflicting arrangement, the clashing styles, techniques, personalities, hung in some cases with consideration for the terms of the bequest, and in others with regard only to the date of the production. There is as yet no museum in America which shows paintings as they should be shown, in distinct schools, in rooms fitted and furnished for the period, with books, musical instruments, etc., of the period. To understand an art one must understand the psychology not only of its creator, but of the society in which he originated and which he served. In our museums as at present managed and organized, the student is compelled to isolate each picture and at some future opportunity to inquire into the circumstances of its production. Nevertheless, and since this is the best available, repeated visits will result in the student's making for himself an intimate history of the art of painting.

Confusion is not so apparent in the European museums because each museum houses as its major attraction the production of the country's own artists, in some instances only that of the painters of the province. (There are of course important exceptions, the Louvre, for instance.) The traveler comes to a city or village fortified with some notions of its history and its celebrities, sees its historic places, types of its inhabitants, etc. When he enters the museum he is already prepared to place the picture in relation to the many social and psychological factors in its making. The student will gain a great deal more from a quick tour through such museums than from a prolonged study of isolated masterpieces of all times and all nations. If such pilgrimages are at all possible, they should be made.

Where the museum student encounters the work of a painter which strikes a sympathetic chord, it will be worth while to obtain a monograph of that painter's life and work. The development of the student's own capacities will be marked by a succession of such ardent loyalties. It is by concentrating upon a limited set of objectives (visible in any one painter's work) rather than by attempting to synthesize qualities taken from many, that progress is made. Originality, it will be found, hatches only after the warmth of first one master and then another. What appears to be native originality will upon analysis be revealed as a logical outcome of a sequence of loyalties (which, of course, express the inclinations of the admirer). The residue of influences is finally compounded by the creative painter into a personal expression. This is the case with such startling innovators as El Greco, Van Gogh, and Picasso, to mention only a few.

If there are deficiencies in museum collections of oil paintings there is in most museums much other material of great value to the art student. Persian and Indian miniature paintings are rich in color harmonies besides possessing the elements of design pointed out. Medieval manuscript illumination also offers line and color pattern worthy of study. The drawings of early Chinese, from the fifth century on, are notable for their beautiful line. (Reproductions may be seen in public libraries.) Egyptian sculpture and relief, Khmer sculpture, Negro fetishes and wood carvings, all created to express racial ideals of beauty, achieved their ends by different usages of the same principles. Each design-concept affords the student an insight into the cultural aims of a civilization.

When some notion of the evolution of styles and expression of peoples and cultures has been acquired by the student of painting, he is prepared to glean the most from contemporary and modern exhibitions. It is believed by some academic defenders of the past that all modern art is an impudent denial of the traditions of centuries. This of course is ignorance. Just as Venetian painting developed certain aspects of Florentine art to a point of great difference in the final products of the two, so modern painting has been an outgrowth of museum art, stressing abstract elements, as was explained. To reject all modern art is therefore to reveal a lack of understanding of traditional forms. (It is true that there is as much bad modern art as bad Classical art.) While not intending this book as a sequel to my *Understanding Modern Art,* it nevertheless supplements the thesis therein developed, namely that all vital art must fulfill two conditions: It must be intellectually related to the art of the museum, and it must express the feelings of a particular society in a particular time. For this reason the student is advised to study the museum first and the contemporary gallery afterward.

It is always fascinating to gain an insight into another's personality. So avid are we for a glimpse of the character and tastes of individuals that we read novels about fictitious beings to enjoy the processes of their thinking and feeling. For the painter and student the one-man show is an open door into the mind and heart of the exhibiting artist. Even a collection of poor pictures will reward the visitor from the point of view of personality.

Books on art fall roughly into three classes, the manual of procedure, the speculative theory of esthetics, and the general criticism written for a wide middle-class public. The manual may teach the student a new technique, discover for him materials and processes, answer questions which have long perplexed him. The esthetic theory may or may not be helpful. It may disturb the painter and throw him into an apathetic state. But if he is intellectually inclined, it may point a direction more definite than the fingerposts hidden in pictures. Orientation is what many students require after they have mastered the difficulties of the craft. The discovery of a theory which awakens his deep response may be really momentous for the painter uncertain of his direction.

The book of general criticism, written to reach a wide audience, has for that reason greater potentialities for affecting art standards. Its appeal lies not only in the simplicity of ideas and expression, but in the literary style of its author and the quality of his prejudices. The art student should read such works most critically, keeping in mind that they are the special reflections of an individual partial to the esthetic credos of the few painters with whom he has been most personally familiar.

Only a few books are here recommended other than those mentioned in the text. This is not because there are not many worthy treatises on art, but because the student will gain a great deal more from making his own discoveries than from checking over a bibliography. We note, however, the following, arranged in progressive order. These should supply a simple foundation upon which to build a personal viewpoint.

Philosophy of Art: (1) *Italy;* (2) *The Low Countries*—Taine

The Florentine Painters of the Renaissance—Berenson

The Venetian Painters of the Renaissance—Berenson

What Is Art (A very stimulating but often perverse speculation)—Tolstoi

ABC of Esthetics—Stein

Modern Painting—Ozenfant and Jeanneret

We leave the question of art books trusting that the adult will not overdevelop esthetic theory at the expense of his production of paintings. There is real pleasure in esthetic speculation but it is not as satisfying as the active, creative thinking-doing required by the blank canvas.

A point made in the Introduction will here bear repeating. The amateur painter must keep steadily in mind the fact that he is in a different class or category from the professional. The artist, we remember, has his blind gift, his unconscious urge, and unerring instinct. The amateur has his cultivated taste, his educated eye, his intellectual motives for doing, his critical faculty for determining the measure of his success. As before stated, it may occur that an amateur will discover in himself a true artist. But candor compels us to state that the instances are rare. Rather than look in the mirror for signs of such metamorphosis, the amateur will be wise to consider himself just an enthusiastic worker until the world discovers his genius.

We take our leave of the reader with the hope that he will find the tribulations of life greatly alleviated by his painting. Practice of the art is at once a recess from, and a heightening of, existence. It widens one's interests, reduces the importance of material values, gives greater attention to the things of the spirit. So it makes for the real pleasure of a richer life. My earnest hope is that the reader will find this book a means, however small, for entering upon this life.

INDEX

165

Paint box, 11, 15.
Palette, arrangement of, 29.
Palette knife, use of, 14, 15.
Pattern, *def.*, 20.
Persian art, 117, 124, 130, 145, 146, 147, 161.
Perugino, 76, 136.
Picasso, 103, 141, 154, 161.
Pigments, list of, 13.
Pissaro, 104.
Plane (s), *def.*, 23, 24.
Poetic feeling, 73, 74, 127, 128.
Pointillist School, 65.
Postimpressionism, 87.
Poussin, Nicholas, 136, 139, 141, 145, 148.
 Eliezer and Rebecca, 138.
Prado, 87.
Purists, 144, 149.

Realism, 24, 50, 51, 116, 121, 124, 136.
Rembrandt, 41, 104.
 Woman Taken in Adultery, 120.
Renaissance, 119, 121, 130, 135.
Renoir, 34, 88, 89.
Reynolds, Joshua, 116.
 St. Cecilia, 116.
Rhythm, *def.*, 113.
Ribera, 104.
Romantic tradition, 119, 122, 124, 132.
Romanticism, 52, 74, 124, 129.
Rouault, 103.
Rubens, 87, 122.
Ryder, 75.

Sargent, 104, 112.
Schwitters, Kurt, 108.
Scumbling, *def.*, 37.
Segonzac, 85.
Shadows, treatment of, 40, 41.
Significance, *def.*, 73.
Silhouette design, 113, 114, 115.
Sorolla, 112.
Speicher, 88.
Static, *def.*, 113.

Titian, 132.
 The Entombment, 132, 135.
Tomita, Keisen, 126.
Turner, 76.
Turpentine stain, 32, 33, 34, 36, 37

Value (s), *def.*, 19, 22.
Vanderpoel, *The Human Figure*, 81.
Van Gogh, 75, 88, 89, 139, 161.
Velasquez, 87.
Venetian painters, 129, 131, 133, 162.
Vermeer, 50, 133, 134.
Veronese, 131.
Vibert, varnish, 43.
Vine, charcoal, 78.
Vlaminck, 103.
Volume (s), *def.*, 22.

Watteau, 139, 140.
Whistler, 104.

Zorn, 112.